HEALING PLUTO PROBLEMS

HEALING
PLUTO
PROBLEMS

Donna Cunningham

SAMUEL WEISER, INC.
York Beach, Maine

First published in 1986 by
Samuel Weiser, Inc.
Box 612
York Beach, ME 03910

Sixth printing, 1992

The material in "Pluto and the Preganancy Trap" first appeared in *Astrology Guide*. Reprinted by permission of Sterling Publications, New York.

Library of Congress Catalog Card Number: 85-52190

ISBN 0-87728-398-2
MV

Cover mandala copyright © 1984 Jeanette Stobie. Used by kind permission of Lightstream Paintings, Glen Ellen, CA.

Printed in the United States of America

The paper used in this publication meets the minimum requirements of the American National Standard for Permanence of Paper for Printed Library Materials Z39.48-1984.

Contents

Why confront Pluto issues; By the time I get to Phoenix.

The meanings of the planet Pluto; An overview of Pluto placements; How to use the delineations; Delineations of Pluto placements; Pluto as a generational planet.

Recognizing Plutonians; How they got that way; The power of the family secret; Emotional secrets and their contribution to isolation; Plutonians in relationship; Sex and the Plutonian; The vengeful victim; Plutonians and the death wish; The hermit, the scholar, and the researcher; The Plutonian as healer, psychotherapist, and reformer; Charts of positive Plutonians; Helpful books for Pluto problems.

The purpose of this book is not only to give insight into Plutonian problems but to find tools to help heal them; The healing crisis; Astrology and Metaphysics; Visualizations and affirmations; Explanation of the flower remedies and how to use them; Light and color therapy; The chakra system; Easy does it; Bibliography of books on healing.

List of Charts

List of Exercises

List of Affirmations

*This book is dedicated to Arnold Panitch
because his communications over the years
have enlivened my life and his help made possible
my entry into the delights of word processing.*

Introduction

Why Confront Pluto Issues?

The topics we will discuss—guilt, resentment, child abuse, and death—are difficult to confront. While talking about these influences of Pluto in workshops, some people grow visibly more and more uncomfortable and have to leave. Typists have broken down and sobbed while working with this material. Given that Pluto topics are painful, is it worthwhile to bring them up? Yes, when you see people who were tormented by guilt come to love themselves again. Yes, when people haunted by terrible secrets break down their isolation and regain self-worth by learning to share them with the right people. Yes, because the purpose of this book is not only to gain insight into Pluto difficulties but to find healing tools for them.

If you are a professional astrologer, it's worth reading this material so you can help clients who will come to you tormented by Pluto problems. While Pluto transits Scorpio, the need to heal these difficult areas will become more and more urgent. Your clients will be confessing their anguished secrets to you, and you need to be able to respond with something other than horror. The information and the healing tools in this book will help you begin to prepare. The bibliographies for each major topic we will discuss tell you where to go to be even better prepared.

And if you, yourself, are a Pluto person, my love to you. A Pluto person is one who has Pluto strong in the chart—for instance, Pluto connected to the Sun, Moon, Ascendant, or Midheaven, or someone who has a number of planets in Scorpio. You *can* get free of the locked in defenses we will be talking about. I won't pretend it's easy. How you got to be a Plutonian wasn't easy. But with consciousness, and with the healing tools described here, you can begin to break down Pluto barriers. If anyone in the world has the perseverance— the obsessiveness, perhaps—to work through a past as devastating as yours, you are that person. The pressures you have withstood in order to survive have left you tempered steel, a diamond in the making. May this book contribute to your life.

By the Time I Get to Phoenix. . .

No, I'm not headed for Phoenix, Arizona. It's the phoenix side of Scorpio or Pluto I'm aiming for—to rise out of my own ashes, reborn. You may be wondering why I wrote a book about Pluto. With Pluto just a degree off the Ascendant, I've never been able to coast, but am perpetually confronted with the need to work on myself and my relationship to the world. It seems more honest to tell you this than to pose as an outside expert, pontificating to "you people out there."

Pluto also symbolizes our relationship to the collective, so in working on my own Pluto problems, I've learned a great deal that has helped the other Plutonians who are magnetized to me. This book is the distillation of that knowledge and of healing tools you can use for Pluto problems. Astrology itself is very healing and should be a great help to you personally and to clients if you counsel others. From my earliest studies, I knew what that Pluto on my Ascendant meant, and it was embarrassing. Pride can sometimes be a virtue, for it made me stop doing those unlovely Pluto things. Hopefully, reading about your own Pluto aspects and house placements will serve the same purpose, of alerting you to your games. It's not easy, though, to read the delineations. More than once, writing about my own aspects, I felt like shouting, "How dare you say that to me!" Yet the conscious awareness itself is healing.

As you read the healing sections of this book, you may wonder, if you are a regular reader of mine, how a nice respectable astrologer with solid psychotherapy credentials got sidetracked into all this weird stuff. . .light and chakras and chants and God knows what else. It was always there, of course, with Pluto on the Ascendant, but I avoided it like the plague. Off beat was okay, but weird, never. Then there came a point thirteen years into my career when astrology died—13 is a Pluto number. For one thing, no one I knew was making a decent living at astrology. For another, it felt like something basic was missing from the astrology I knew. Once the chart diagnosed the client's problem, where was the solution? I decided to quit and look in earnest for a new career.

During that time, I had been meeting weekly with a very fine psychic named Andrew Ramer. We started a project about the spiritual dimensions of alcoholism which evolved into a book on addictions—quite wonderful and powerful material. Next, Andrew channeled some material about *healing* addictions and their after-effects, and I began to try out the material on recovering alcoholics. Before long, both my healing group and individual clients were thriving on it. Sometimes being too impatient to wait for our next session, I started channeling myself. (It feels like I was led, blindfolded, step by step, since my fear of these developments was so pronounced.)

Next I found a notice about a class on herbs in an adult education program and saved it—it would be just the thing for Andrew. He was too busy, and somehow, almost without volition, I was on the subway headed for the class. The third week, the teacher introduced the Bach Flower Remedies for emotional problems, and I began studying them. They have been an intrinsic part of my work for more than four years. Later it became clear that I had already found my career change. These tools, and others subsequently learned, added an important dimension in which the problems so readily diagnosed by the chart actually had some solutions. Astrology had not died after all, it just moved on to another level!

CHAPTER ONE

Understanding Pluto
in Your Chart

The planet Pluto is naturally connected with the sign of Scorpio and with the eighth house. These three categories have some common interest in such matters as birth, sex, death, power and transformation. Power and how to deal with it is a major Plutonian issue, both at the individual level and for humanity. In this chapter, and throughout this book, we will be exploring the psychological complexities of Pluto, both in the birth chart and by transit. Where the manifestations are mainly negative, we will seek ways of healing or ameliorating the difficulties Pluto represents. This chapter provides delineations of Pluto's house position and aspects in the birth chart, as well as some thoughts on the meaning of Pluto in various signs. (For the novice or beginning student, the Appendix tells you how to find your own Pluto placements.) If you have a number of Pluto aspects (or if the eighth house or the sign Scorpio is strongly represented in your chart), you would also get further insight by reading Chapter Two. A Plutonian personality is someone with Pluto very strong in their chart, as described in the introduction.[1]

---

[1] Aspects to the Sun, Moon, Ascendant, or Midheaven involving Pluto, or someone with several important planets in Scorpio or with a strong eight house indicates a "Strong Pluto."

Themes you might expect with Pluto placements are guilt, resentment, the desire for control, spite, or revenge. Yet no one seeks revenge without being deeply hurt, so there is often a horror story of some kind connected to the Pluto placement in the natal chart. For instance, you may see the after-effects of a crucial death or abandonment manifesting in a tendency to develop symbiotic relationships, alternating with periods of isolation. Although some people are more fundamentally affected by Pluto defenses than others, we all display some Pluto traits in the areas of life Pluto touches.

An Overview of Pluto Placements

Much of what will be discussed in the following pages is aimed at the person with a difficult Pluto. If your Pluto is well aspected (having only trines and sextiles) or if your Pluto is not particularly strong, this material may not apply to you to any great degree. Yet you may find that even the weakest placements (such as Scorpio on the cusp of a house with no planets in that house) apply to some of the difficulties you have. If so, reading the comments would give you some insight, even if you are not involved in some of the more drastic behaviors of that placement. Whether your Pluto is strong or weak, you may squirm at some of the readings, yet confronting the truth is the beginning of change. Once is not enough, though—we have to keep on knowing, and keep on confronting, until the games we play are exposed so often they embarrass us and we have to let go of them. Admitting them to others accelerates the process.

We are often obsessed with the matters of the house or planets involved with Pluto's placement in the natal chart. And yet, what we can't let go of, we wind up perpetuating. The same negative pattern may come up in our lives over and over, and with each repetition we are more fixed on it. Where we have been hurt or betrayed, we expect betrayal, so we select people who will betray us and then set up the betrayal by our expectations. Even a decent person who is subjected to constant suspicion can be pushed to say, "You don't trust me? If that's all you think of me, then I'll go ahead and do it!" Thus we create our own self-fulfilling prophecies.

One dynamic which can be the cause of an obsession is a tendency to get into power struggles in matters related to Pluto's house or aspects. Such fanatical insistence on winning can paradoxically lead to bitter failures. This often begins as a power struggle with a parent (or other important authority figure) in childhood—someone who placed great emphasis on the matters of Pluto's house and tried to push the child to succeed there. If the child succeeded, the parent won. In order to spite the parent and win the battle, the individual had to LOSE in the matters involved with Pluto's house. The failure is perversely regarded as a moral victory. This dynamic has led me to call the house where Pluto is placed "the fail for spite house."

Alternately, the parent may have taught the child that he or she would never amount to anything in matters of that house, so the person extracts revenge by failing consistently in ways that embarrass the parent. There is a death's head smile as the person laments their failure. . ."See, Ma, you were right!" Some people freeze that area out of hurt, controlling needs and feelings so rigidly that even friends wouldn't guess it was important, yet they are not free of it. Along with this could go a sour grapes attitude—"I wouldn't want it anyway"— and a sense of moral superiority over those who do succeed.

Another bind occurs when the person buys into the parent's belief that the matters of Pluto's house or aspects are so powerful that it would transform (and control) the life if he or she succeeded in it. As a result, an exaggerated degree of power is assigned to that area of life. Because of the power given to the Pluto department of life and the power struggles being carried on there, the person can wind up being controlled by the thing he most wants to control. He is powerless to succeed and yet powerless to let go of it, until he transforms himself. Paradoxically, when the Pluto area is healed and loses its power over you, it is an area where you can manifest a considerable degree of constructive power. In these patterns, you may recognize a bit of the scorpion's sting, for you win the battle at the expense of harming yourself.

The person with a difficult Pluto placement can be a scorpion in that area of life, acting out venom on others, usually in a covert or twisted manner. I call this syndrome the *vengeful victim*, in that here is where the person feels wronged, yet feels most justified in returning that wrong to others. A man with Moon in Scorpio, for instance, may feel greatly wronged by his mother, and may somehow feel justified in taking his rage out on any woman who gets close to him. Not all of us are vengeful victims, of course, but many of us do like playing the victim at times, and if the Pluto areas of your life are difficult ones, you might think about whether this dynamic is operating to some degree.

There may be the deep, dark secret in the Pluto area of life that makes you feel you cannot be open with others. We all have Pluto somewhere and we all have secrets. Readers may be relieved to know that we will not discuss the sexual implications of the various Pluto placements. So often, the deep, dark secret *is* a sexual one. But it's not about sex, really. When there is sexual difficulty or sexual obsession, the real issue is often power. The same critical issues of betrayal of trust, abandonment, guilt, and resentment may play into the power sexuality has.

How to Use the Delineations

The following delineations consider Pluto in various aspects, house placements, and in some of its signs.[2] They are arranged in house order, with similar placements grouped together. For instance, Pluto in the third house is grouped with Pluto/Mercury aspects and with Mercury in Scorpio, because all have similar effects. No two aspects are alike, but there are similarities that can help the astrologer discover similar themes. For example, in each of the combinations Mercury concerns are paired with Pluto concerns, resulting in some common themes. Where one of the combinations is markedly dif-

---

[2] The appendix provides further details about Pluto aspects, and includes information so students can locate Pluto in the natal chart.

ferent or has an important individual theme, it will be treated separately. Because I do not hold with the traditional rulerships of Venus for Taurus or Mercury for Virgo, they are omitted.

The strength of the combination is not the same for all those grouped together. The approximate order would be:

Pluto in difficult aspect to a planet

Pluto in a house

A planet being in Scorpio

Scorpio planets in a house

Scorpio on the cusp of a house

Pluto in a sign

Apart from putting Pluto in the house first, the order of placements in a particular delineation is arranged in the approximate strength I judge them to have, as it does occasionally vary. The aspects referred to are mainly the hard ones (the conjunction, semisquare, square, sesquiquadrate, quincunx, or opposition). Sometimes even a trine from Pluto can give you some of the described traits. The conjunction would be the strongest of all, the sextile probably practically negligible in effect. (Not listed, but also possibly similar might be the planets and signs in the eighth house.)

Delineations of Pluto Placements

Given what we have said about the relative strengths of the placements, if you have Scorpio on the cusp of a house and nothing in that house, you would not expect it to operate nearly as strongly as having Pluto in the house, or Pluto in aspect to the planet naturally associated with that house. The effect might be fairly mild, compared to the delineations, which are written with the stronger combinations in mind, yet they would doubtlessly be there in a less dramatic and thus perhaps less conscious form if you examined yourself. Let's look at how the combinations work.

PLUTO IN THE FIRST HOUSE

All strong Pluto aspects to the Ascendant, Scorpio Ascendant, Scorpio planets in the first house. (Pluto/Mars aspects will be treated separately.)

This is a difficult placement, particularly when Pluto is close to or aspecting the Ascendant. These people would probably be classed as Plutonians. (See Chapter Two.) Power struggles may be expressed by the physical appearance. These people manage to look dramatically different in a way that alienates others—such as wearing black leather jackets, sexually provocative clothes, having a weight problem, or dark, brooding expressions. You can almost hear them saying to a parent, "You can't control the way I look." Since the first house is one of the health houses, it is crucial to work on guilt and resentment issues, as over the years the energy could translate into serious physical problems. (Healing this sort of problem is discussed in Chapter Four.)

The Plutonian personality may alienate others, as these people may go around with chips on their shoulders, radiating resentment. They may stringently control emotional expression, not trusting the world with any important information, constantly scrutinizing everything. When angry or resentful, they may withdraw into solitude or become loners. Relationships may be based on doing too much for others or binding others symbiotically. When that fails, isolation is the result. The reason for this lack of trust might be a very early betrayal of trust, abandonment, loss by death, or other difficult family conditions. (The first house shows defenses we adopt because of the family environment and other early events.)

This is a powerful placement when used constructively, for these individuals could have a great impact on their environment. As they become comfortable with the use of power, their influence on others could be very great. It is one of the signatures of the healer or psychotherapist, for these people can see right into the heart of the problem and empower others to heal themselves. These people may also be mediums, aware or unaware.

Pluto/Mars Hard Aspects

Mars in Scorpio

Anger is very difficult to express, and is held in under pressure until it becomes an all-permeating resentfulness and brooding, because these people feel anger has the power to destroy, even to kill. Some violent trauma may have occurred, or perhaps there were terrible undercurrents of resentment in the early environment, with violence an unexpressed threat. At the very least, there is a belief that anger could destroy relationships, or open conflict could lead to abandonment. Since the power of anger is exaggerated, these people control it at all costs, yet walk around with it constantly. Others feel the anger and the dishonesty about it, and may become resentful in turn, and the Mars/Pluto people may ultimately be abandoned, just as they feared. As Mars/Pluto people become more comfortable with anger, they can heal long-standing resentments, freeing them to use the energy in a powerful way. Controlled use of this energy gives a tremendous capacity to focus. The energy may also be used for healing or to accomplish other prodigious feats.

PLUTO IN THE SECOND HOUSE

Scorpio planets in the second, Scorpio on the second.

Power struggles can focus on money, which was doubtlessly an important issue for the parents. When the parents gave, they exercised a good deal of control, so giving was colored with resentment or had strings attached, in order to keep the child close or dependent. As a result, these Plutonians equate money with control, and may either have a great deal or none at all.

Some people fail for spite by having chronic financial difficulty. This may arise when parents predicted the child would never amount to anything financially. There can be great resentment of people who do have money. (One client called wealthy people "Philistines.") Some may balk against the things you have to do to earn money, confusing managemental cooperation with control. Resentment about money and the control it exercises over life can poison any attempt to become financially solvent.

Poverty itself may become a mechanism for control in relationships. That is, these people may become symbiotically involved with others who "help" them, creating dependency in order to control or not be abandoned. Their lack of money is always the final word, the trump card they play. ("I can't do what you want because I don't have the money.") Sexuality can be a ploy in the game, but then both parties come to resent having to pay that way. In lieu of an actual person to be dependent on, second house Plutonians may draw on government aid, perhaps with some underlying pleasure at "getting back at the system." Resentment toward those with money may also lead less ethical individuals with this placement to "liberate" money or goods from their employer, who is viewed as corrupt and exploitative.

The flip side of the coin would be seen in individuals who earn a decent amount of money, but who do it to maintain control of relationships or the environment. These Plutonians are the "helpers" who get involved with people who couldn't manage without their financial aid. This seemingly gives second house Plutonians the upper hand in their relationships (because who holds the purse strings calls the shots) and also creates the feeling that they can't be abandoned because they are needed so much. Eventually, they resent having to earn money for these reasons, and in the end neither the relationship nor the work is truly successful. Resentment poisons all efforts, and they don't earn as much as they could, nor do they feel loved for themselves.

If you put together the key words for Pluto and for the second house, you get earning power, and that is a constructive interpretation of this placement. People with Pluto in the second who work to get rid of the negative Pluto dynamics of resentment, spite, guilt, power struggles, and control related to finances can wind up being extremely successful. They can be money magnets or magicians when it comes to transmuting resources into wealth. To be successful, failing for spite has to be given up.

PLUTO IN THE THIRD HOUSE

Pluto/Mercury, Mercury in Scorpio, Scorpio on the third.

These people believe words are so powerful they have the power to destroy. They are extremely careful to control what they say, lest they give away some information that another might use to harm or control them. This condition occurs when at least one family member had a black belt in tongue karate, a sarcastic or scathing individual they were powerless to resist. This might well be a brother or sister, probably older, who was so overpowering that the Plutonians learned to keep quiet.

As adults, third house Plutonians can either be afraid of verbal abuse or be verbally abusive and sarcastic, agreeing that the best defense is a good offense. Another possibility is that words can be the focus of a power struggle—as long as they don't give you their words, they have the upper hand. In relationships, they may withhold communication. As employees, they may withhold paperwork or other important information. As students, they may be the ones who won't turn in their papers, asking for extension after extension. Words can also be used to manipulate, with great effectiveness.

People who use this placement constructively are perceptive and deep in their thinking and communicating. They are gifted at seeing others' motivations and can penetrate deeply into any problem. They can use words to heal, going straight to the heart of the matter. They are fine analytic writers and teachers. Rather than being manipulative, they can use words to influence and empower others for good purpose.

PLUTO IN THE FOURTH HOUSE

Pluto/Moon, Scorpio Moon, Scorpio planets in the fourth house, Scorpio on the fourth.

This is a very Plutonian person, especially when Pluto falls near the fourth house cusp. One parent, most likely the mother, was powerful, intrusive and controlling. When one parent was outwardly domineering, however, the other may have been more subtly manipulative—"It's you and me against that monster." Often there are great undercurrents of resentment in the home, particularly resentment of the child's needs, or of the necessity for nurturing. Sometimes a grandmother exerted great influence, in the manner of a matriarch. There may have been an actual abandonment, such as a death of a parent figure, or there may have been the constant threat of abandonment if the child did not behave. Perhaps everyone was mourning a death near the time of this child's birth, so the mother was in a melancholic state and had little to give an infant.

With a Scorpio Moon or Moon/Pluto aspects, there may be difficulty trusting women, resentment of them, or manipulation to make women symbiotically dependent in order to avoid abandonment. A parent with this placement may resent having to nurture children, yet overcompensate or symbiotically bind children by doing too much for them. A parent may hold on to children in a life or death manner, feeling that this is at least one relationship where he or she will never be abandoned. Conversely, the scars left from the lack of loving nurturance in childhood may be so deep that this individual resolves never to become a parent.

When people have Pluto or Scorpio in the fourth, the adult home may become a battleground for power struggles; or, to avoid repeating past family patterns, these people may decide to live alone. It can be hard to cope with living with anyone, unless this type has absolute control of the situation. "My house is my private turf, my secret sanctuary, and I can't really bear to share it." It is essential that people with this placement respect their need for privacy and solitude, knowing that even when they live with others, they still need time alone. As they heal childhood traumas and resentments, it will become easier for them to live with someone else. The home life then becomes the wellspring of regeneration, giving them healing energy to take out into the world. They have the ability to heal themselves of early traumas and, when they do, they may share what they learn with others who have been similarly wounded.

PLUTO IN THE FIFTH HOUSE

Scorpio planets in the fifth, Pluto prominent in Leo, and Scorpio on the fifth. (Pluto/Sun aspects will be treated separately.)

With Pluto or planets in Scorpio in the fifth house, at least in older generations, there is often a situation of being forced into marriage because of a pregnancy. Even within marriage, pregnancy might be used as a means to gain control of the relationship, for instance to ensure that the mate doesn't leave. Since this is not a very successful way to control, these people often wind up resenting or spoiling the children in an attempt to make up for not wanting them in the first place. Brats are very often unwanted children who've been raised this way; the parent has given excess power to the children and over-indulged them because of guilt. Such children resent how they are being used, learning early to manipulate and maneuver both parents. The children can also be seen as a means to power, or can be one parent's ticket to never being alone, so the ties become symbiotic (Cancer Rising often has Scorpio on the fifth, so this placement helps explain Cancerian smother love.)

On the other hand, people with this placement may refuse to have children at all. When the "inner child" has been denied by a parent, these children grow up to fear or resent the demands that their own children would make. They fear parenthood would take over their lives and leave nothing for themselves. There is also the unwelcome issue of power that parenthood would bring. Childlessness can also be a form of revenge toward either the mate or the parents, a refusal to confer them immortality.

With Pluto in the fifth or prominent in Leo, one parent may have been overawed by the child's creativity and have seen it as a means to wealth and power. Like pushy stage mothers, they may have gone too far, and talent became the focus of power struggles. This happened to many Pluto in Leo people, as it was the first generation with enough leisure time and affluence to develop the creativity innate in all of us. Talent can become the focus of many power struggles, especially with lovers who think love is power that will transform and bring out budding genius. Romance and transformation are all mixed together for people with any of these combinations. "Let me love you so I can make you over in my own image." Or vice versa. For more insight into the romantic functioning of this placement, read Pluto in the seventh and eighth, as they are similar.

Pluto/Sun Hard Aspects

To a lesser degree, Sun in Scorpio. When Pluto is prominent in Leo, you may see some of these dynamics.

Here the toxic authority figure is usually the Plutonian father, often a harshly domineering man. Because of his own power and ego needs, he could not afford to praise his child, as though anything the child did well diminished him and anything the child did poorly reflected on him. With such a father, there is no winning.

When used negatively, this placement combines Leo's egotism and desire for attention with Scorpio's will to power. The self-concept is bound up in *Being Somebody*. Self-hatred can be an issue if these people aren't having an impact on their world, and they sometimes employ ruthless or questionable tactics in order to be important. With Scorpio/Pluto extremism, they feel that if they aren't Somebody, then they're nobody and life isn't worth living. They can resent people in the spotlight or rush into battles when egos are threatened. If power struggles are lost, self-hatred is multiplied.

Paradoxically, when these people are able to let go of the need to be the center of attention, when power is no longer important, they can actually become very powerful people for a good cause. The power comes from an endless resourcefulness, radiating from the center of their being, light from the inner Sun that never burns out. The Sun/Pluto aspect shows the potential to transform the self. When something needs to be worked through, these people don't let up until it has been handled. After healing the self, the capacity to heal others with similar problems will manifest itself.

PLUTO IN THE SIXTH HOUSE

Scorpio planets in the sixth, Scorpio on the sixth, possibly Pluto in Virgo.

This often indicates individuals who are obsessed with work to the point of being workaholics. These people serve, yet resent being subservient; work compulsively, yet resent having to work so hard. Such people believe jobs are their own personal avenues to power, and so maneuver to be the power behind the throne by becoming indispensable. Since this will to power is easily recognized by both the boss and co-workers, these individuals are mistrusted. Power struggles ensue as well as resentments and vendettas with coworkers, and these people may leave one job after another on bad terms.

The sixth house is another health house, so Pluto there natally (or by transit) indicates the possibility of illness coming about through stored-up resentment. Illness may be the only means available to stop the work compulsion. When work has failed as a way to power, the sixth house Plutonian may control others through illness, becoming the invalid who makes everyone dance. Symbiosis is assured: someone has to take care of them. Most people can't abandon an invalid— they'd feel guilty!

Used constructively, this placement indicates people who continually transform themselves through work, recognizing that work and work relationships are a microcosm of all of life. Any situation arising on the job can be used as a means to confront and deal with the parts of themselves that need changing. Work can become powerful in transforming life; and these people can also become powerful transformers through their work. This is another signature of healing ability, sometimes developed due to the stimulus of an illness.

PLUTO IN THE SEVENTH HOUSE

Pluto/Venus aspects, Venus in Scorpio, Scorpio planets in the seventh house, Scorpio on the seventh, possibly Pluto in Libra.

Love can be an obsession, and symbiosis with the loved one is sought. A subatomic reaction of possessiveness, resentment, guilt, and power struggles can occur. When that alienates the loved one, this Pluto type may flip over into isolation, deciding not to have any more relationships. Some may continue to have a relationship in their head with the last one who did them dirty, being haunted by it. Others may elect to stay single, because this type equates love with control and they don't want any part of that.

For many with this placement, love equaled control in childhood, and unless they submitted to the power of the parent, there was the threat of withdrawal of love and approval. Perhaps there was an actual abandonment or death which made them fearful of losing love, so they cling very tightly and try to make themselves indispensable. There may have been a symbiotic relationship with a parent like that described under Pluto in the fourth—it's you and me against that monster. (To some extent, these dynamics may be true of Pluto falling into the other relationship houses, the fifth and the eighth, as well.)

If Scorpio is on the tenth, then Pluto falling in the seventh may show a parent who bound the child too tightly or who may have betrayed the child's trust in a serious way. Sometimes, the parent of the opposite sex was so overwhelming, dominating, or seductive that this Pluto placement finds it terrifying to form intimate relationships. (There is often a change for the better in relationships after that parent dies.)

Another dynamic is that relationships and transformation are mixed together. These Plutonians may fall in love in order to make the loved ones over, and the loved ones may resent both the insistence on change and the implied inequality of the relationship. Power struggles may develop and ultimately lead to abandonment. The "patient" may even get worse, out of spite. Or, the Pluto person may be the patient and fall in love with a powerful mentor.

When this placement is used constructively, relationships can become an arena for transformation, both for the self and the loved one. In order to be whole, these people may have to go through a process of working through hurts and resentments about each love affair that ever went wrong, in order to let go and forgive. When these people heal their relationship difficulties and learn to let go, this placement would also become a good counselor, particularly a marriage counselor, using the counseling relationship and a capacity for love as a healing force.

PLUTO IN THE EIGHTH HOUSE

Scorpio planets in the eighth, Scorpio on the eighth, possibly Pluto in Scorpio.

Sex is a sticky issue for people with this placement. They have been taught to give it an enormous power in their minds, so it becomes a fearsome thing. (We in our culture have all given sex an exaggerated amount of power, but the eighth house Plutonian carries this belief to an extreme.)

These people may feel that if they become involved sexually, the partner will control them. As a result, they may think twice about getting involved at all; yet they are passionate people, so it is hard to avoid what is so powerful. In sexual relationships, they may seek to have the upper hand at all costs. Giving or withholding sex becomes a means of control, and bed can become a battlefield where other issues of power in the relationship (or in the outside world) get acted out. When resentments or mistrust build up in the relationship, sexuality can be frozen. Even after the end of a difficult relationship, this type may remain frozen and unwilling to open up to someone new. With this placement, the deep, dark secret is often very much present.

The eighth house is also a money house, so dynamics similar to those outlined under Pluto in the second may operate. Shared resources are not an easy issue for such people, being an area where there could be a good deal of mistrust and a stringent need to maintain control. Inheritances and other dynamics of the grief process might lead to bitter battles. (See Chapter Six.)

Here, also, death is very much a question and regarded with fear and fascination. Sometimes, the child may have lived in a household where there were many deaths, or even more powerfully, where there was an on-going threat of death, which is more difficult to deal with. Perhaps Pappa had a bad heart, and the family was forever watchful. This Pluto type could have a tremendous fear of death and live life from the perspective of, "I could die at any minute."

The constructive use of this position is as a healer and possibly as a medium. There is a great ability to regenerate self and others. When sex is cleared of its heavy emotional overlay, it can become an important means to rejuvenation and regeneration. When money is not the source of a power struggle, this position may indicate good earning power or the ability to empower others to success.

PLUTO IN THE NINTH HOUSE

Pluto/Jupiter aspects, Jupiter in Scorpio, Scorpio planets in the ninth house, Scorpio on the ninth.

This shows a deep, analytical mind, yet this person may balk at completing a higher education. This type resents having to get a degree to succeed, as getting one would mean their parents won. Many such people go all the way through school, then somehow fail to complete the last semester, the last course, or even the last paper. This is a great revenge, maddening to parents who so much wanted their child to have an education, which was seen as a magical key to getting somewhere.

This may be seen as a fail for spite ploy, because these people also believe that education is powerful and life -transforming, and that without it they won't get anywhere. Where Pluto is, one tends to give over power, so one is stuck there—"damned if you do and damned if you don't." Resentments can be displaced onto society. One highly intelligent man with this placement who had just one course to go to complete a badly needed degree expressed his resentment toward society. I shocked him by saying, "You know what? Society doesn't care whether you finish your education or not! Society doesn't even know you exist! The education is only for you." Startled into clarity by this deliberate shock therapy, he went on to finish his degree. (Similar resentments and self-spiting patterns may exist toward The Law or The Church.)

When these people work through the resentments that are getting in their way, Pluto here can be an excellent placement. These people are actually born scholars and researchers and would get great satisfaction from studying on their own. They could also be powerful teachers who could get to the heart of abstract issues, using the power of the mind to release others from the bondage of ignorance. Knowledge IS power, and the right use of knowledge could transform the world.

PLUTO IN THE TENTH HOUSE

Pluto in hard aspect to the Midheaven, Pluto/Saturn hard aspects, Scorpio Midheaven, Scorpio planets in the tenth, at times a prominent Saturn in Scorpio.

These placements show very difficult conditions with authority figures and most likely a parent who was oppressive, controlling, and perhaps even abusive. The result is deep-seated resentment toward people in power (maybe toward the whole world) and a determination never to be under the control of someone else. The bind is that these people are also very success oriented, and it is difficult to succeed if they are forever setting up battles with the powers that be. The scorpion's sting means that they are usually the ones who wind up getting hurt. They may be playing with the Big Guys, who are born strategists, while their own resentments lead them to make ill-considered moves.

Parents with this position who are not able to be powerful in the world may act out power needs on their children, repeating, in fact, what was done to them. Pluto in the tenth shows a critical, highly ambitious parent who respected nothing but BIG success and was never pleased with child-sized successes. The parental curse "You'll never amount to anything," may have been frequently heard, and this

Plutonian may go through repeated humiliating public failures in order to get even. This depth and degree of the fail for spite game is not fun!

These people may be stubbornly resistant to healing, because all healing in some way represents being under someone else's power. Possibly it is best undertaken alone. Working through the exercises on resentment in Chapter Four could be very important. A healing career is quite possible—and they will have to heal themselves in the course of their studies! People who are freed from the negative manifestations of this placement, who are able to work with power in a clean way, can have a strong impact on the world, bringing about healing and reform.

PLUTO IN THE ELEVENTH HOUSE

Scorpio planets in the eleventh, Scorpio on the eleventh.

Here the bogeyman is not the powerful parent but the peer group these people tried so hard to belong to as teenagers and yet never could. For some, sex was the price of belonging. Others chose to isolate themselves rather than submit to the control of the group—after all, teenagers demand more conformity than parents ever could. Resentment over what went on in school can get in the way of belonging as an adult. Power struggles can interfere with friendships, which may be entered into on the possessive, symbiotic level we see so often with Pluto. Others may stay isolated, even as adults, because it is difficult to trust. Group membership may be difficult also, as these people are drawn into "organization politics" as a means to power.

Group therapy or self-help groups could bring about transformations regarding personal alienation. As issues of trust and resentment are worked through, the capacity to be a powerful group leader could emerge. These people may be drawn to groups which aim at social reform, environmental control, or healing. Friendship can become the area where these people are transformed, for becoming involved with other Plutonians who are not afraid of intensity can work for mutual healing.

PLUTO IN THE TWELFTH HOUSE

Scorpio planets in the twelfth, possibly Neptune in Scorpio, Scorpio on the twelfth.

Repression of emotions can cause either self-destructive behavior or physical illness, since this is one of the health houses. Here illness can serve the purpose of allowing these people to stay secluded from a world that seems too powerful, too dangerous and untrustworthy. Illness can be a way to control others, and this is also true of the emotional illnesses of the twelfth house. Have you ever had to tiptoe around someone who was severely depressed all the time and felt controlled by their seeming fragility? Addiction, a twelfth-house ploy, can also be used to control emotions and keep others safely at bay.

These people may repress an urge-to-power and yet control in round-about ways they little understand. For instance, being the seemingly helpless victim also serves to conceal the power urge—have you ever "rescued" some poor helpless soul who later took over your total life and all your energy? No doubt you learned that victimhood is powerful! (Please understand that there are legitimate victims, but here we are talking about the illegitimate ones, the ones who are forever drawn to these situations thinking that their suffering is some sort of moral victory.) Unconscious fascination with power can also lead to contacts with underground characters, negative psychism, and various unsavory scenes where power is used in a murky way. Healing submerged resentment can go a long way toward lifting this position out of its negative manifestations into the constructive, thus Chapter Four (on guilt and resentment) can be useful. In the house of secrets, the deep, dark secret is ever the possibility, and revealing it in the right therapeutic places can release you from its power.

The constructive use of this placement is in its capacity to delve into the unconscious and heal deep-seated emotional problems. Thus, it is a frequent placement for those working in the field of mental health. Likewise, people who have suffered from an addiction and been able to stop have the most power to help other addicts. This is also a mediumistic or psychic position, and one where the study of dreams can be very useful. Spiritual healing is another strong possibility.

•••

In looking at the delineations of Pluto's house and aspects in your own chart, there is doubtlessly something you don't agree with, yet in some cases the readings may bring up things about yourself that you don't like. You may have glimpsed residues of old traumas, abandonments, or betrayals that are still affecting your life in a negative or painful way today. What can you do to transform these difficulties? In Chapter Three, you will find suggestions, exercises, tools, and books to read that can help you.

Pluto in a Sign
as a Generational Influence

Until recently, Pluto was designated as an "impersonal" planet and its sign was considered of little significance, as it affected masses of people. The house and aspects, it is true, show Pluto's most obvious effects on the individual, and yet I am coming to see, as a number of other astrologers are, that the sign Pluto is in can have a profound influence on our psychology, albeit more internal than outward. While it is more common to refer to Pluto as a generational planet, one's generation (and powerful world events that take place in formative years) can have a pronounced effect on personal values, beliefs, and behavior.

For instance, much has been written lately about the "ME" generation, the narcissism of people of a certain age. This corresponds astrologically, it seems to me, with the Pluto in Leo generation, born 1937-1958. Leo is a narcissistic sign, and Pluto in Leo people can be self-obsessed when that planet is prominent. Combining the symbolism of Leo and Pluto can give you a picture of the possible psychological effects of that placement. This generation, for instance, was the first to be strongly affected by the mass dissemination of psychological concepts, yet these ideas are primarily directed toward the self. You hear endless conversations about MY analyst and MY Oedipal complex and MY dreams. When that generation got interested in the occult and spirituality, it was MY guru and MY psychic powers and MY dreams.

The Pluto in Leo generation was also the first with enough leisure time and affluence to develop their innate creativity. As a result, that generation contains a million frustrated actors and singers waiting to be discovered, a million painters who are certain they'll make the Louvre if they can just get a show, a million would-be authors with ideas that are sure to hit the best-seller list if they'd only find a publisher. All of this with the lazy Leo assumption that such recognition is a birthright rather than something to sweat for.

A valuable corrective is to recognize that nature is wildly prolific in order to ensure its own reproduction. It creates a million sperm for each one that is strong enough to make a baby, a thousand seeds for each one that has the stamina to make a plant, and a hundred creative people for each one who has the discipline to develop the talent. As Rainer Maria Rilke said, "If I don't manage to fly, someone else will. Spirit wants only that there be flying. As for who happens to do it, in that He has only a passing interest." Unless we are willing to totally dedicate our lives to that talent, we may not write our name on history. But talent IS transformative, and it can be powerful as a means of self-knowledge and self-expression. It can be a source of healing for ourselves and other people as well.

Much time has been spent on the Pluto in Leo generation because it is the dominant adult group in the world today. Lest you think the generation is hopelessly self-centered for all time, remember that during the eleven years Pluto is in Scorpio, it will be making hard angles (squares) to the Pluto in Leo placements and this could be a time of mass transformation, in which the work these self-obsessed individuals have done on themselves should come to be shared with others, creating a whole generation of psychologically aware healers.

The Pluto in Cancer generation is quite different from the Pluto in Leo generation, and this, I believe, was partially the source of the generation gap so much talked about years back. (A study I recently read says that this gap does not exist between young people today and their parents.) The Pluto in Cancer group, scarred by the experience of the Great Depression and two World Wars, was very security conscious, holding on tight to family and traditional values. This clashed with the hedonism and individualism of the Pluto in Leo generation, whose main commitments were to the self and the current romance. (Planetary placements during the 1960s, such as Uranus and Pluto in Virgo, made social reform a pressing desire.)

Pluto in a sign shows your generation's obsessions, being where you take yourself too seriously and can go off the deep end. Michael Lutin has observed that Pluto in a sign introduces compulsive behaviors to keep the matters of that sign from dying, yet the behaviors themselves contribute to the ultimate destruction. For instance, he pointed out that the refrigerator was developed during Pluto in Cancer as a way to preserve food, yet once that occurred, women didn't have to spend all their time at home cooking, so they went out to work and the family was never the same.

Among a great many other things, our generation's Pluto sign may be an indicator of our attitudes toward sex. These values come from the general public and from the media at the time we are young, but get imprinted and become the "shoulds" we try to live up to. For Pluto in Leo, sex is a performance, supposed to be dramatic, romantic. It's an ego trip—"I am so great I can get all these sex partners, and

I can make you come." The Pluto in Virgo people will probably ultimately find their parents immoral and adopt a much more chaste attitude, more monogamous, partially in response to the spread of fearsome sexually transmitted diseases. They do have Neptune in Scorpio, however, so they may first be sex addicts, as we all were when they were born—"Make Love not War" and "Free Love" were the slogans of the time. Note that music is ruled by Neptune, and Neptune in Scorpio people have adopted sexually explicit music.

On the whole, however, it is too early for us to be able to make intelligent statements about the Pluto in Virgo generation, much less Pluto in Libra or Scorpio. The effects of Pluto in a sign are so long range and there can be so much enlightenment or endarkenment of the natives of that generation, we cannot tell what the end will be. We do not even, for that matter, know how Pluto in Leo people will react to the Pluto in Scorpio square to their natal Pluto.

Pluto and the Unfolding
of the Collective

The outer planets (Uranus, Neptune and Pluto) are closely linked in their effects on the world, collaborating for the unfolding of the collective. It seems that Neptune goes through a sign first, somehow dissolving and corrupting the matters associated with it, making the concerns of that sign an unreachable dream. It is almost as though it infects all of us with an illusion that we addictively try to attain, rather like a vapor trail that Pluto years later clears up. Uranus currently follows Neptune, popularizing and disseminating the illusions, making them available to the masses.

Pluto goes through a sign some twenty–eight years after Neptune and destroys the illusions of Neptune in "X" generation. For example, the Neptune in Virgo generation (1921-1942) was born under the shadow of unemployment and poverty of the depression, so this generation came to idolize work, as though it were somehow divine. Yet, these people have had to suffer both addiction to it, as in workaholism, and disillusionment when it did not make them live happily ever after. Work became meaningless during the time Pluto was in Virgo (1958-1971), encompassing the 1960s—the tune in, turn on, drop out era, when the work ethic was abandoned.

While Neptune was in Libra (1943-57) relationships became Hollywoodized. We began looking for happily ever after, the perfect and eternal romance, with someone as beautiful or handsome as a movie star. The more we sought this dream, the less we could deal with real people in relationships, but were perpetually itching to go find romantic nirvana, someone to lift us out of the human condition and into the divine. During Pluto's transit through Libra, these illusions crashed and relationships suffered from having to see reality.

Pluto in Libra intensified resentment about unequal relationships, so that what actually got destroyed were relationships where power was unequal. Maybe it is all Grand Plan and we ARE moving toward equality, but we need therapeutic isolation from one another in order to feel we don't need one another to survive. Thus, when we get back to relating, it will be on a different basis. After Pluto in Libra has destroyed our illusions about relationships, so that they became progressively embittered, we may now all need to learn how to be alone (a possible interpretation of Pluto in Scorpio). Or, we may defend ourselves against loneliness by intensifying all the Plutonian defenses—the control, manipulation, symbiosis and power struggles. Except in the end, it will be clear that they don't work.

For the Neptune in Scorpio generation (the children of the flower children) and the collective consciousness since that time (1957-71), our illusions, fascinations, and addictions have tended to be sex, wealth, and resentment or cynicism about the corruption of the power structure. The eighth house represents debt and Neptune illusion or slavery, so we've all been living in a fantasy land with credit cards the magic wands. Under the influence of this placement, we've collectively come to think that sex was so important that it controlled our lives. Ads playing on sex were used as a way of manipulating us into buying beyond our means. We've been living a set of illusions about sex and reproduction too, with unneeded hysterectomies and chemical or surgical intrusions into the birth process making doctors rich. The use of destructive chemicals for birth control gave us an illusion of sexual freedom, yet the physical, emotional, and spiritual costs are beginning to be apparent. The current prevalence of sexually transmitted disease (like Herpes and AIDS) is already causing people to reassess their "liberated" sexuality. Illusions we bought into when Neptune transited Scorpio will be reevaluated as Pluto moves through Scorpio.

Many astrologers have remarked on the way the form of the planets follows the function, how the peculiarities of their construction say something about the way the planets operate in our lives. Once more this is true when we think of the unusual irregularity of Pluto's 248 year orbit. At some points in its path around the Sun, it spent as long as thirty–two years in a sign, whereas during recent history it stays in a sign only eleven years. This is celestial mechanics, objective reality, and yet it may be part of the acceleration of change in our lives. We all feel things are moving too quickly, decaying too fast; we all have a sense of too many endings, even of time running out. Consequences seem to happen faster, and yet paradoxically our life spans are increasing as we conquer once-deadly diseases.

These ideas about the effects of Pluto and the other outer planets are only preliminary. Astrology seems headed in the direction of uncovering much more about the meanings of these placements, yet I would love to see a good historian with a background in political science and economics tackle this subject. We are at a rather exciting point in the development of astrology, and we can look forward to knowing a great deal more about the meanings and historical correlations of the outer planets in the signs.

CHAPTER TWO

The Personality and Character of the Plutonian

Let's state clearly that this is not a book about Scorpios, but about Pluto in all of us, how to understand it, and if Pluto is not working well for you, how to heal it. This chapter demonstrates the best and the worst of the Plutonian. Insights and healing tools are presented for Plutonian types. Because the Plutonian who has worked through the negative is in the best position to help the rest of us, special attention and help is given to Plutonians here.

Recognizing the Plutonian

First, it might be well to define what we mean by Pluto people. If you look at their charts—that is, if they *let* you look at their charts, as secretive as they are—you would find Pluto aspecting the Sun, Moon, Ascendant, or Midheaven. Usually, it is more than one of these, mostly in hard aspects like the conjunction, semisquare, square, sesquiquadrate, quincunx, or opposition. Sometimes Pluto aspects a number of other planets, or the person has key placements in Scorpio, which Pluto rules. Having several planets in the eighth house can also produce some of these effects.

If you don't have the chart, or if you don't know that much astrology, how would you recognize the negative Plutonian? There are certain personality traits that tend to go along with these chart patterns, although not all will be present in a single individual, of course. If you are a Plutonian and some of these traits emphatically do not fit you, just let them go and take what is helpful and descriptive of you personally. What will be given is a composite picture, based on working with a great many Plutonians over the years.

Plutonians who are negatively inclined are often very guarded and rigid, afraid to let others get close. Never revealing much about themselves, nonetheless they know everything about you, having drawn it out of you in the guise of helping. Plutonians often look intense and can have a mournful appearance that drives others away. Many are bitter and resentful, obsessing about the past, projecting the attitude, "Look what they did to me." They are often mistrustful—it was for them that the t-shirts were designed that say, "The paranoids are out of get me," or the others that say, "I don't get mad, I get even." Or, black t-shirts that say nothing at all, for Plutonians are often dressed in black. Even their humor is black. How many Scorpios does it take to change a light bulb? None, they'd rather sit in the dark.

There are Plutonians who operate predominantly on the positive level—healing, transforming, transmuting themselves and those around them. Never content with the superficial, they look deeply into life and people, having a natural gift for understanding what makes people tick. Some few are to the manner born, through exposure to parents who were positive Plutonians. More often, however, the positive Plutonian comes to the ability to heal through the necessity of healing the effects of difficult childhood or life circumstances. Many have survived extremely harsh and traumatic backgrounds which might have crushed a lesser soul but gave these resilient souls the strength of diamonds.

Plutonians have the gift, as well as the compulsion, to find methods of dealing with the painful events in their history, and thus will work on resolving the past. In short, many positive Plutonians began as negative Plutonians and worked their way up, through persistent effort. Most of this chapter is devoted to understanding negative Plutonians and the remainder of the book to tools for healing Plutonian difficulties we all face.

Plutonians are born counselors, so they tend to attract troubled people. However, Plutonians of the more negative variety make themselves indispensable, subtly convincing you that you'd be helpless without them. You can't understand why you've come to resent them and you feel guilty, since they do so much for you. Somehow the balance of power in the relationship has shifted so that you're doing things their way all the time and feel guilty if you don't. Women more often than men resort to this kind of manipulation in order to have power. Power and control are the underlying issues of the planet Pluto, pure and simple. Since Pluto people are neither pure nor simple, however, their attempts to control come out in disguised ways—often disguised even from themselves. Control is achieved by such subtle means as manipulation, emotional blackmail, "helping," and guilt.

Another characteristic of negative Plutonians is their way of dealing with emotions. Being in command of emotions is to be in command of the situation, or so Plutonians reason. Feelings are seldom shown, especially those where control could be threatened—anger, neediness, or vulnerability. Plutonians disclaim anger, yet inwardly seethe. You sense it and are bothered, but they insist, "No, no, nothing is wrong."

Then one fine day, the Plutonian tells you that you've been doing X for months, it drives her wild when people do X, how could you be so insensitive, and she never wants to see you again. You are devastated, since you had no idea X was a no-no, and since she has led you to be so heavily dependent on her that you think you can't manage on your own. You are dead as far as she is concerned, for there is no resuscitating the relationship. You aren't the only one—this scenario is repeated over and over in the lives of Plutonians. It may, in fact, be the only way they know how to relate.

How the Plutonian Got that Way

I don't mean to imply that Plutonian people deliberately *choose* this painful pattern. It is helpful to remember that the defenses which cause such pain for these adults once made it possible for them as children to survive a difficult and often hostile environment. These children had to deal with abandonment, death, resentment, guilt, secrets, sex, or the revenge motif. Often, there were traumatic betrayals of trust or threats to survival—bad family situations. As we will see in Chapter Five, a strong Pluto is common among children of alcoholics, abused children, and incest victims. Others might have lost a parent through death or bitter divorce, or they may have been children who suffered greatly at the hands of powerful adults.

Often, there was an overwhelming mother who misused her natural power over the child, being either overtly domineering or covertly manipulative. Sometimes one parent is harsh and punitive, while the other, seemingly weaker, is actually more controlling. "It's you and me against that monster, so you'd better stick close and do just what I say." The "good" parent can actually wind up being more of a problem, because anger against the domineering parent is clear cut while the saint/martyr parent creates guilt and seemingly un-merited resentment.

Often Plutonian children are unwanted, although the parents may overcompensate and cover up by spoiling them. Sometimes the parents have so many problems and are so enmeshed in power struggles with one another that the child is simply an added aggrava-tion. Sometimes the pregnancy itself was no more than a ploy. This happens, for instance, in "forced marriages" or when a marriage is just about to fall apart and the wife "just coincidentally" winds up pregnant at the critical moment. Such ploys are not especially suc-cessful these days, but even when they glue the parents together resentment is created. The child may bear the brunt of the parent's anger, especially if the child resembles the mate.

Another situation which may create a Plutonian is grief in the family at an early age. A death may occur within the year before the child's birth, or sometimes within the year after. The household is in mourning, and the infant absorbs grief as part of its character struc-ture. Such a child may have been conceived to replace the lost loved one. It seems almost an instinct, beyond reason. Even I, who never wanted children, found myself crying over babies in the street while my mother was dying. As we'll see in Chapter Six, a bereaved person is angry, and that anger can be felt by the infant and taken as a personal message regarding self and the world. In addition, grief leaves little energy over to attend to life, so the infant's emotional needs may be resented, or not met, or met by fits and starts. Conversely, when the lost person is crucial to the mother (such as a parent or a child), she may cling symbiotically to the Plutonian child to make up for the loss.

Also likely are one or more unresolved, deeply mourned deaths or losses. Plutonians seem to collect more than their fair share of deaths, and each new one may trigger remnants of older grief. As Dylan Thomas said, "After the first death, there is no other." Mourning may need to be completed in order to allow the Plutonian to let go of melancholy.

Sometimes there is only the recurrent *threat* of loss or abandonment, a threat that damages the child as much as an actual loss. I am reminded of my short-term group about mothers and daughters in which each of the seven members had a Moon/Pluto aspect, and I, "coincidentally," was going through a Moon/Pluto transit. Intrigued, we probed to find out what each had in common. All the women had been continually threatened by their mothers as they were growing up—either she would die or wouldn't be there when they got home from school. The group was short-lived, because during our second meeting the phone rang to tell me that my mother died. This shocking confrontation with the thing they had been threatened with all their lives was so traumatic that none could continue. (I do suspect, however, that they needed to confront the reality of their mothers' eventual death, and that was the true purpose of the group.)

The Power of the Family Secret

A family therapist I worked with, Dr. Dick Auerswald, talked about "the secret" that was always at the heart of the family pathology. The secret twists family members up in their relationship to one another and the world. The Plutonian person is often one who lived in a family full of secrets, ugly skeletons in the closet. Living that way made the Plutonian feel tainted, as though acceptance outside the confines of the family could only be won by concealment.

What sorts of secrets? You must understand that we are now in an age of much more openness than even twenty years ago when the adult Plutonian's sense of self-worth was being formed. Not that long ago, tuberculosis was a scandal not unlike leprosy, epilepsy was the kiss of death as far as having a career or a mate, and if you had an insane or retarded relative you hid that fact. With Pluto in Scorpio, much more taboo subjects, like incest and child molestation, are more openly discussed, but even now they are terribly difficult secrets to live with.

A strong Pluto is common in children of alcoholics, and this disease is still a shameful secret. The parents won't admit the alcoholism, although the behavior may be obvious, so it is not even all right to discuss within the family. Thus, family members deny the problem and engage in a conspiracy to keep the outside world from knowing. Teenagers, in particular, want so badly to be like everyone else that they hide the fact that a parent drinks. Carrying this burden, the children become afraid to let outsiders know them, even as adults. (Books for children of alcoholics are listed in the bibliography.)

As the child grows up, the family secret retains its hold, but the isolation it creates inclines the Plutonian to develop other secrets. These are mostly desperate things done to find love and overcome that awful sense of being alone. Since Pluto has a great deal to do with sex, some of the secrets are sexual. Or, deep resentment can lead to hostile actions that are also guilty secrets. (Chapter Four will give more insight into these actions and ways to purge the guilt so you can love yourself.)

In the Anonymous programs, they say you're only as sick as your secrets, and it's true that secrets can make you sick. They can even cause cancer if they're malignant enough. If you have a secret that's twisting you up and you need to be free, there's no way to do it but to find the right people to share with. Use your common sense, mind you, but share it. Secrets lose their power when you tell them. I've been listening to people's secrets professionally for almost twenty years, and out of all those secrets there was only ONE that shocked me. I won't tell you what it was, but I can guarantee yours is nothing compared to it. If yours is as bad as all that, they'll make a TV movie about it within the year. That's what Pluto in Scorpio is about—an end to secrets!

Emotions as Secrets
that Contribute to Isolation

Plutonian people are often loners, for even surrounded by other people they can feel alone in a crowd. One major reason is that they hide their emotions so not to be betrayed by them. In doing so, they come to believe that what they are feeling is so removed from the human condition as to be alien. Any number have confessed to a sense of being from another planet.

All Plutonian traits develop for good reasons. There were seething, painful emotional undercurrents in the home which periodically flared into the open. The child had to be perpetually alert to jump out of the way of the blow that was coming. The blow wasn't always physical. Sometimes it was verbal, sometimes even psychic. Maybe it was the threat of abandonment, disapproval, or loss of love. But the threat was there, and the child needed to monitor it continuously. Some of the feelers the child used to keep tabs on the situation were: acute awareness of body language, tone of voice, minute facial changes, and even psychic perceptions. (As adults, Plutonians make extremely perceptive counselors. Sensitivity like that can't be taught in a psychoanalytic institute.) The feelers were necessary, because truth was taboo, and survival depended on knowing what was going on. Most especially, the child had to monitor the mother's emotional condition, so it was best not to stray too far. The child who sees things, however, is often punished if he dares to speak of his perceptions.

What goes on is somewhat like the story of the emperor's new clothes. Some con artists convinced the emperor they were weaving him clothes of a material so delicate that only the most refined, sensitive people could see it, when of course they weren't weaving anything at all. Soon the emperor and all his court were oohing and aahing over his beautiful clothes, when in actuality he was stark naked. There was just one little boy in the crowd who spoke the truth—the emperor had no clothes on. Did you ever wonder how the story really ended? Being a Plutonian myself, my bet is that nobody thanked him for it. More likely, that little boy got his behind tanned when he got home! That little boy was doubtlessly a Plutonian, and he got smart real quick and shut up about what was going on. However, if your parents lie about what is happening, you come to distrust and resent them.

When the Plutonian ventures outside the family and its dangerous emotional undercurrents, the sensitivity continues. Unspoken feelings are regarded as threatening and perilous even in situations where the red alert is unmerited. A second kind of mistrust begins, because people constantly lie about feelings—never mind that they primarily lie to themselves. The child senses the discrepancy between what is being said and felt, and if he dares to speak up about it, he may be punished or ostracized. When this happens enough, the young Plutonian comes to feel that people are not to be trusted with feelings. Simultaneously, the youngster may also feel strange for having these apparently unacceptable perceptions. Since lies continue in social situations throughout life, adults become wary of speaking out. Awareness of the lying and of being different creates a painful isolation.

Another contribution to the loneliness is that not only do people react badly when you reveal what THEY are feeling—one could, after all, respect a desire for privacy—but they also react badly when you reveal what YOU are feeling. If it's a difficult feeling, they'd just as soon you stifled it. And, if it's a Plutonian feeling, like grief, jealousy, or resentment, it's really taboo to talk about; once, maybe, but people are likely to move away from you if you are *too intense*. Try telling your New Age, Spiritual, or Transformed buddies that you'd seriously like to kill your wife who has just left you, and then listen to the sound of the phone not ringing. Or, if your pals are Plutonian themselves, they will tell you what to do to get over these feelings and get annoyed when you don't. You finally learn to shut up, and the feelings become all the more awful for not being shared.

Group therapy is extremely helpful for unspoken emotions. You can imagine that the last thing Plutonians want to do is reveal themselves in a group of *strangers*. One on one with someone we are paying to listen isn't so bad. We can pretty much control the situation—therapists don't say much anyhow, and we can always fire them if we don't like their reactions. I hated group therapy every single week for over a year, yet it was one of the strongest healing experiences I have ever had. I was shocked out of my proud/angry sense of alienness by being with people I didn't choose and couldn't control. They were so different from me and my values that I would never have chosen to get close to them. Hearing them express the same reactions I was having, I was forced to conclude (you wouldn't believe how reluctantly!) I was human after all and not so very unique. Self-help groups also revealed how much I was like others, but one can be silent within such groups, never reveal much, and move away when it becomes too intimate.

The Plutonian in Relationships

What a strange thing loneliness is and how frightening it is. We never allow ourselves to get too close to it; and if by chance we do, we quickly run away from it.[3]

At a point of fascination with transactional analysis, I decided each Venus position could be identified by the games people played to avoid intimacy. Especially striking were those tied to Pluto with the relationship houses (the fifth, seventh, or eighth). This would apply to Venus in Scorpio, also to Pluto aspects to the Ascendant/ Descendant axis, and probably to all Plutonians. These people have two main games, and one so readily shifts into the other that it's hard to discuss them separately.

The first is, "Til death do us part," with all its potentially sinister ramifications. Plutonians don't form relationships, they take hostages! They are so intense about love that they genuinely believe it's a life and death matter. They are not above a one-night stand, because they can be quite passionate; but the morning after they evaluate you as a life long partner and make an irrevocable decision. If they like you, you're it. No easing in and exploring each other, then making up your mind. Possibly, with their keen insight into people, that's all the time it takes to make a valid psychological assessment, but nonetheless it can scare off folks who need longer to make a commitment. Once in a relationship, it is such a relief after the painful loneliness that they become obsessive and possessive. Fearing abandonment, they attempt to bind the lover with mechanisms described earlier. Out

[3] J. Krishnamurti, *Commentaries on Living*, Quest, Wheaton, IL, 1967.

of desperate fear, they often tragically create the abandonment they work so hard to avoid, for they wind up being suffocating.

After such a desertion, the second game comes into play: "I've been burned before." They may go deeper into isolation, since that gives them total control over their environment. Some of them never try again, playing the game of "loved and lost" or "soul mate." They hang on to the old, dead love and visit the cemetery regularly. Bitter recriminations go on and on against those who eluded their grasp, even though the loved ones were essentially driven away.

The pattern can be self-perpetuating. For instance, a Pluto person might have experienced a betrayal he cannot let go of. Such a person expects to be betrayed again and often selects someone very likely to betray him, ignoring other kinds of people. ("They simply don't turn me on.") Then by words, behavior, and body language, his lover is maneuvered into fulfilling those cherished expectations. After a while, anyone would get tired of the accusations and conclude, "If that's all you think I'm good for, I'll go ahead and do it!"

After playing "I've been burned before" for a while, loneliness builds up to a painful level again. When someone eventually ignites the embers of the desire for intimacy, the new love has a problem, for she will have to jump through hoops to prove she's not like that other one. Once the Plutonian starts to believe even a little bit, we're right back to "Til death do us part!" The exercise for opening the heart center given in Chapter Three can help ease this intensity about relationships.

The Plutonian and Sex

Plutonians can be very passionate people, sometimes even obsessed with sex. Like all their feelings, sexual desires and sensations can be intense—one of the advantages of being a Plutonian! They can be gifted lovers, as keen sensitivity to what is going on with others, even mediumistic abilities, can help them zero in on what to do for their partner's utmost satisfaction. Their passionate, intense, mysterious look can also make them highly desirable. Plutonians, in short, are hot.

That's the good news. The bad news is that sex is a complex issue for Plutonians, full of emotional pitfalls. The need for power and control is part of the reason sex can be compulsive. "Scoring" is winning, and Plutonians are bent on winning at all costs—even when the sexual conquest is not to their advantage personally, socially, or professionally. In fact, the more risky it is, the more of a secret it has to be, the more it turns them on. Often, Plutonians will be powerfully attracted to social inferiors, relishing the feeling of being on top. Or, conversely, they may go after people with power or money, seeing either as an aphrodisiac. They may also be attracted to dangerous people, engaging in a battle for control by using sex. Sexual conquest may also be a form of revenge against the current partner, a past partner, or a parent.

Sex, in short, serves many purposes other than physical release. For one thing, they don't feel alone any more. Yet, the essential isolation of Plutonians is such that loneliness returns quickly, so sex may become a constant need. Sex may be used as a hedge against abandonment. Plutonians may also use intimacy as a defense against intimacy. That is, lovemaking leaves little time for talking, so Plutonians may keep you so busy that you don't notice the lack of verbal communication.

Eventually, however, something in you *does* notice, some part of you rebels at being a sex object, you catch on that you are being controlled. You start feeling alone in the midst of all that intimacy, and you feel shut out. You may come to resent doing it their way or feel used by the fact that you are always fulfilled and totally exposed, while the Plutonian never loses control or lets you fulfill him or her. By that time, you are either hooked by the other relationship games the Plutonians play, like making you dependent, or you may leave. The Plutonian is abandoned again.

The reasons for sexual compulsiveness and control go back to the origins of the Plutonian personality. Incest or child molestation may be part of the Plutonian's history, so sex and misuse of power coexisted from the child's earliest experiences. Perhaps the home atmosphere was charged with sexual energy, and the child was overstimulated at a young age by being too exposed to adult sexual activity. (Didn't Freud, that old Plutonian, come up with the theory of the primal scene as part of the origin of neurosis?) One or both of the parents may have been promiscuous or unfaithful, and this fact shaped the Plutonian's picture of relationships and sexuality. Equally often, the sexuality wasn't overt, any more than other seething emotions in the home, but the child absorbed the frustrated sexual undercurrents, perhaps being closely tied to an unconsciously seductive parent. Where the child felt unwanted or unloved, lacking real intimacy, he or she may have taken whatever intimacy was available and may have been sexually active earlier than most young people. Given the combination of one or several of these conditions, intimacy becomes sexualized for the Plutonian, who may not know any other way to be close to people.

If you are a Plutonian and are wondering why you aren't such a hot number, why you've been celibate these many years, or why, when you do consent to have sex you don't enjoy it, the answer may go back to some of the difficult situations that made you a Plutonian in the first place. The betrayals of trust, the intrusions on your body and emotions, or abandonments may have been so severe that you have real difficulty in opening up and letting go of control this way. Perhaps you are holding on to loads of resentment against your mate or a past relationship, the frozen anger making you frozen sexually as well. The work on resentment in Chapter Four can help with that, and some of the other healing tools given in Chapter Three can help with sexual functioning. You *could* be just as sexy as those Plutonians described earlier, trust me!

The Vengeful Victim

Please let me begin by saying that there are REAL victims. As you will see in Chapter Five, people who have had overwhelming power used against them feel powerless and thus can perpetuate their own victimization in subsequent relationships. These unfortunate people deserve nothing but compassion.

Where we have Pluto in our charts, we can all sometimes play what I call the *vengeful victim*, but negatively inclined Plutonians can devote years and considerable energy to it. In such situations, these people feel wronged, yet feel justified returning that wrong to others. People filled with hate because of things a parent did twenty, thirty, forty years ago can extract revenge from everyone who tries to get close now. It doesn't make sense, of course, but these people feel morally correct and self-righteous.

Naturally, none of this is conscious—all the Plutonians are aware of is bitterness over what was done. Yet they hold on to the resentment, and by holding onto it, it is perpetuated, as in the example of the lover who gets pushed into betrayal by the repeated suspicions. The payoff is that the Plutonians get to say, "See, I was right! People aren't to be trusted. Betrayed again!" This is said with a death's head smile that shows they somehow think they won in this exchange. Actually, the best revenge is living well.

Acting the victim can become a ploy in the revenge. The wrong is played up to the hilt, so others feel somehow guilty and responsible, as though they should make up for what was done. Woe be unto the person who tries to help the vengeful victim—and these types are seductive to many of us who need to rescue! It's a lot like trying to take a thorn out of a lion's paw. When you get hooked into such an interaction, just when you feel the sorriest, you realize you've been stung, maneuvered, used. New York, for instance, is full of starving artists who feel victimized because society doesn't recognize their talent (Pluto in Leo) and who are bitter that they can't earn a living that way. They extract revenge by playing the victim role to the hilt, finding lovers who feel sorry for them and compelled to pay the rent.

Plutonians and the Death Wish

Sigmund Freud, who had Scorpio Rising and Pluto on the Descendant, invented the concept of the death wish as a universal human urge. Maybe that idea is valid, or maybe Freud mainly drew other Plutonians to himself—the rising sign does determine what we draw to ourselves and the Descendant says a great deal about our partnerships. Was Freud haunted by a death wish that he projected onto the rest of humanity, or do we all have it? (Freud, whose chart is presented later, also had Neptune in the eighth house, which could show the tendency to see death as an escape.) Negative Plutonians, nonetheless, often have a strong death wish. Some have an ambivalence about living, an anger that they have to be here, and a lack of acceptance of being compelled to live, along with suicidal fantasies.

As described in the book *Life Before Life*, Helen Wambaugh hypnotized many hundreds of people, many of whom did not believe in reincarnation or survival after death. Nearly all remembered events in the period before birth, including knowledge of the life task and the selection of their parents, in which they participated. There were some individuals, apparently Plutonians, who did not wish to incarnate again, who were born more or less against their will and were very angry about it. Some remembered miscarriages their mother had beforehand in which they were supposed to be born but withdrew. I ask Plutonians who evidence ambivalence about living if there was such an event in their family before they were born, and they often reply, startled, "How did you know that?" (The mother's psychic perception of the child's unwillingness to live could be one reason a mother would cling possessively to a child, in the dynamics of Plutonian development discussed earlier.)

Ambivalence about living may stem back to early exposure to grief. Unresolved and unconscious grief, let's say over losing a parent figure, can lie behind a wish to die. Also, if the parents were in mourning, they themselves may have been ambivalent about this child's existence, and the child, feeling unwanted, may have concluded it was better never to have been born. Where conditions were traumatic, the child could early on have absorbed an attitude that life was not worth living. For instance, the rate of teenage suicides for the generation born in the middle to late Sixties with Pluto conjunct Uranus in Virgo has been extremely high, doubtlessly because this represents extremely difficult home situations when the aspect is prominent (e.g., aspecting the Sun, Moon, Ascendant, or Midheaven).

Regardless of its source, Plutonians have to resolve this ongoing ambivalence in order to live fully. Books on reincarnation and survival seem to help, since Plutonians can begin to see that there is more to life; that even if life is difficult, there is purpose to it. Such books also discuss the after-effects of suicide and the probability of having to repeat the lessons of this life if that way out were taken. (See

Chapter Six, where we discuss how this knowledge helped a Plutonian let go of a suicidal preoccupation.) Clearing out deep-seated resentments about the past with the tools in Chapter Four also helps Plutonians feel life is worth living.

Pluto—The Hermit, the Scholar, the Researcher

It is not that we love to be alone, but that we love to soar, and when we do soar, the company grows thinner and thinner until there is none at all. . .We are not the less to aim at the summits though the multitude does not ascend them.
— Henry David Thoreau

Thoreau's words remind me of the eagle/phoenix side of the Scorpio nature, for Plutonians are also loners in a more positive sense, focused so totally on achieving some necessary purpose that they have little time for frivolity. They resemble the Tarot card, The Hermit (see Figure 1). One of our first and bravest people to soar was Amelia Earhart, whose solo flights made her a legend. As you can see from

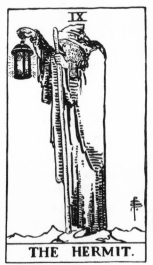

Figure 1. The Hermit, from the Rider-Waite Tarot Deck. Reprinted by permission of U.S. Games Systems, New York. Further reproduction forbidden.

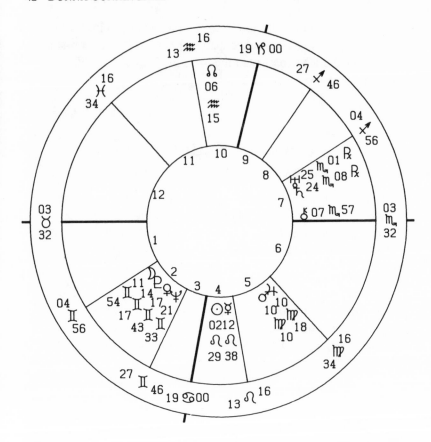

Chart 1. Amelia Earhart. Born Atchison, Kansas, July 24, 1987, 11:30 PM CST, tropical, Placidus. Data is reproduced from Lois Rodden's *Profiles of Women*, AFA, Tempe, AZ, 1979, p. 131. Used by permission.

Chart 1, she has Pluto conjunct the Moon, Venus, and Neptune in the air sign Gemini, plus the conjunction in Scorpio of Uranus (the planet associated with aviation) and Saturn (the planet of achievement and self-discipline). Her chart is Plutonian, and her death was a mysterious disappearance on a flight rumored to have been a spy mission.

For some time I had been using the metaphor of Madame Curie laboriously sifting tons of pitchblende to harvest a small amount of Uranium to illustrate the hard, committed, solitary work Plutonians

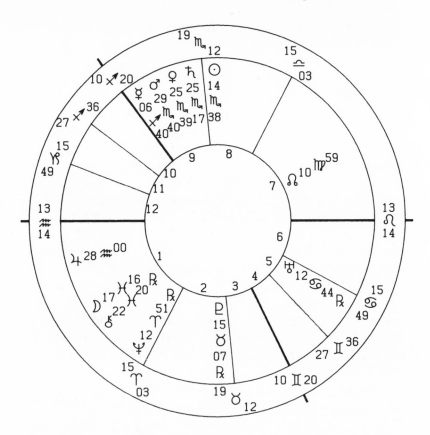

Chart 2. Marie Curie. Born Warsaw, Poland, November 7, 1867, 1:06 PM, tropical, Placidus. Data from Lois Rodden's *Profiles of Women*, AFA, Tempe, AZ, 1979, p. 226. Used by permission.

are capable of. Finally it occurred to me to look at her chart. (See Chart 2). She has four planets in Scorpio, including the Sun in the eighth house opposite Pluto and a strong conjunction of Mars, Saturn, and Venus. Mars/Saturn conjunctions have a very bad reputation and in Scorpio neither planet is very much sought after, so I can imagine what a gloom and doom astrologer would have told the Madame if she were unscientific enough to consult one. "Forget it. All your efforts will come to naught!"

I once asked painstaking astrological researcher Michel Gauquelin what occupation went along with Pluto Rising or Culminating
(i.e., on the Midheaven). He said it was for the researcher, and that he
himself had it. Madame Curie's Pluto is not in the Gauquelin sectors,
yet she is a Plutonian and a researcher of the highest order. Nuclear
energy itself seems Plutonian, in that it is used for healing, especially
for the Plutonian disease of cancer, yet also has the power to destroy
our world. As befits her Plutonian chart, Madame Curie is posthumously one of our most powerful individuals, in that her dis-
coveries have changed the course of history.

It is also important to consider that the isolation suffered by
Plutonians may be karmically necessary. Punishment is not implied
here. Isolation may be a condition which some require in order to
develop their abilities to the fullest or to achieve an agreed-upon life
purpose. It may be necessary to focus on some singular activity,
rather than being immersed in the daily needs of family or other
relationships. The life purpose may be one which is so demanding—
and yet one the world needs so badly—that considerable personal
sacrifice is needed. For this sacrifice, Plutonians deserve our love and
support. Most of us retain little awareness of our karmic life tasks, so
the Plutonian may be left only with the pain at being alone. Post-
humous fame seems to go along with such far-reaching pursuits, and
yet this thought is small consolation.

Although it is painful, isolation also gives you the self-
containment to go deeply within. It is not so easy to hide from
yourself when you are alone, nor is it so necessary to pretend as when
you are with others. One of my treasured friends, a Sun/Pluto conjunction, said that by the age of twelve he had recognized that the life
path he chose would often be a lonely one. Delving deep within is not
for the ordinary person, nor does it receive much social validation. It
also requires solitude to do the painstaking analysis of self and life
typical of both the psychologist and the spiritual seeker.

Being set apart, even though it is difficult, gives you the perspective to understand your culture, why it is the way it is, and how to
correct its problems. Psychologists, reformers, and others who have
an urge to make an impact on problem-solving in the world are often

Plutonians. Not being as immersed in the culture as the ordinary individual, the Plutonian is not so controlled by its values and can explore many new dimensions. As Dag Hammarskjold said, "Pray that your loneliness may spur you into finding something to live for, something great enough to die for."[4]

The Plutonian as Healer, Therapist, and Reformer

Plutonians can make superb therapists. They are keenly aware of everyone, understanding every nuance of tone, movement, word choice, and what is not said as well as what is. A difficult home situation may be the training ground for alertness, and even though it developed as a survival mechanism, this skill makes Plutonians excellent diagnosticians. Through the pain experienced, Plutonians make mighty efforts to heal themselves and in so doing develop the courage to confront unconscious emotions and motivations. Through self-analysis, they can also develop the capacity to analyze others. If we do indeed choose our charts and our parents, as reincarnational studies suggest, then perhaps Plutonians select such rough circumstances to impel them in the direction of helping people.

As a result of background and experience, Plutonians have a natural gift for psychology. The chart of Elisabeth Kübler-Ross, the advocate for the dying, is presented in Chapter Six (Chart 17, page 130). She is a psychiatrist with the Sun and Moon conjunct Pluto. Another example is Sigmund Freud (see Chart 3 on page 46), whose chart will be referred to in several chapters because of his impact on our thinking. Freud is clearly a Plutonian, in that he has Scorpio Rising and Pluto directly opposite the Ascendant. The dynamics of Pluto can be seen in his career, both in the positive sense of healing and in the negative sense of power and control.

---

[4] Dag Hammarskjold, *Markings*, Knopf, NY, 1964, p. 72.

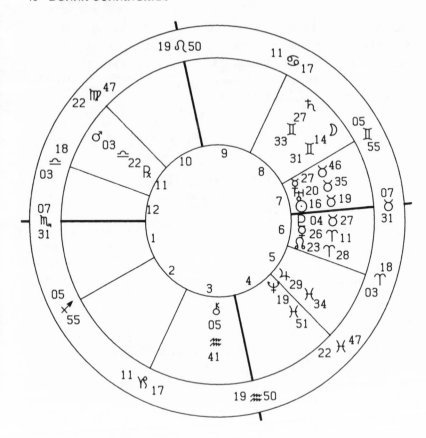

Chart 3. Sigmund Freud. Born Frieburg, W. Germany, May 6, 1856, 6:21 PM, tropical, Placidus. Birth time recorded from father's diary according to Lois Rodden's *American Book of Charts*, ACS, San Diego, CA, 1980.

Psychology alone is not the extent of Plutonians' capacity to heal. Plutonians who purify resentment and other toxic conditions can develop the capacity to use healing energies of a more subtle sort, such as the techniques introduced in this book. Power in its purest sense, when the desire to control is absent, can be used to transmute matter or energy, so Plutonians can develop the ability to heal mind, body, and spirit—hopefully some combination of the three. Ellen

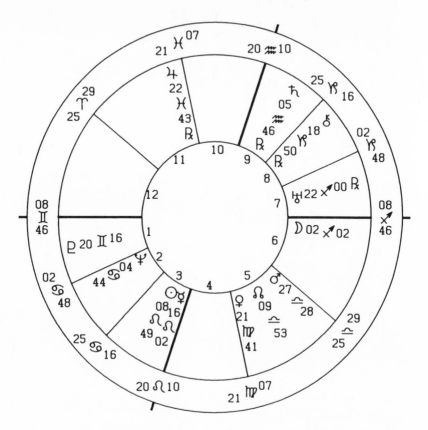

Chart 4. Ellen Yoakum. Born Hillsboro, Texas, August 2, 1903, 1:20 AM CST, tropical, Placidus. Data from Lois Rodden's *Profiles of Women*, AFA, Tempe, AZ, 1979, p. 138. Used by permission.

Yoakum (see Chart 4) is an example of a healer whose abilities were well-accepted and recognized by the medical profession. She had a Grand Cross (a stressful but dynamic rectangle) with Pluto in the first, Jupiter in mystical Pisces, Venus in health and service-oriented Virgo, and unconventional Uranus in Sagittarius, the sign of the preacher.

Since Pluto is closely allied with the collective, Plutonians can also have a strong desire to heal on a mass level; thus many reformers have a

Chart 5. Gandhi. Born Porbandar, India, October 2, 1869, 7:11:48 AM LMT, tropical, Placidus. The birth data is questionable according to Lois Rodden in *The American Book of Charts* (ACS, San Diego, CA, 1980). Even with a questionable birth time, readers should note that the t-square involving Pluto would be in effect, and it is this t-square aspect that indicates his powerful motivation for reform.

strong Pluto. One example is Gandhi, whose efforts to free India entailed great personal sacrifices and that Plutonian capacity to thrive under pressure (see Chart 5). His chart has a t-square (a dynamic triangle) with a Pluto/Jupiter conjunction in Taurus, Moon in Leo in the tenth—showing his capacity to inspire the public—and a Venus/Mars conjunction in Scorpio. He also has Mercury in Scorpio near the Ascendant.

Moving from Negative to Positive Uses of Pluto

If you are a Plutonian type, you may be wondering how you can move away from the negative and painful uses of Pluto to the positive and constructive ones. Psychotherapy, of course, would help you understand yourself better, and hopefully this book will provide you with many insights. More importantly, Chapter Three will introduce practical tools which can be used to purge guilt, resentment, controllingness, and other negative Pluto traits.

Books for Adult Children of Alcoholics

Black, Claudia. *It Will Never Happen to Me*, M.A.C. Printing and Publications, 1982. A book by the pioneer in the field of treatment for adult children of alcoholics, specifying the personality traits and problems that accompany this family problem. (Order from ACT, Box 8536, Newport Beach, CA 92660, and ask to be on their mailing list for seminars.)

The NACOA Network. Box 421691, San Francisco, CA 94142. Newsletter of the growing network of groups and services for adult children of alcoholics.

Seixas, Judith S. and Geraldine Youcha. *Children of Alcoholism: A Survivor's Manual*, Crown Publishers, N. Y., 1985. Written by two authors who have made substantial contributions to the field of alcohol education. Seixas has also written fine books for teenagers and young children with alcoholic parents.

Other Helpful Books for Plutonians

Friday, Nancy. *My Mother/My Self*, Dell, N. Y., 1978. A powerful book on the symbiosis between mother and daughter, very useful in attaining consciousness into the pervasive effects our mothers have on our lives.

Hoffman, Bob. *No One Is to Blame: Getting a Loving Divorce From Mom and Dad*, Science and Behavior Books, N. Y., 1979. Full of helpful insights and processes to get free of programming and old hurts and angers toward parents.

Keyes, Ken. *A Conscious Person's Guide to Relationships*, Living Love Publications, St. Mary's, KY, 1979. A transformative book which looks at the addictive qualities in relationships, including that of control and being right. Help in deprogramming yourself for better relationships.

Kushner, Harold. *When Bad Things Happen to Good People*, Avon Books, N. Y., 1981. An attempt to look at the question of why if there is a God, tragedies happen to people.

CHAPTER THREE

Healing Tools
for Pluto Problems

We have just discussed a number of problems common to Plutonians which, sooner or later, will confront all of us in some way. Having a better understanding of where these difficulties come from may be helpful, yet insight without direction can be depressing. Increasing self-knowledge without increasing the power to change can even add to self-hatred. Some people say, "If I understand why I do it, why can't I stop?" This chapter will introduce you to the tools you can use to change yourself. Because Pluto, Scorpio, and the eighth house all have to do with healing, a secondary goal is to inspire more Plutonians to become healers. In healing yourself, you learn the craft of healing, and this may lead to the desire to help others. With Pluto in Scorpio, there should be a resurgence of the healing arts as a normal and natural part of life.

The Healing Crisis

The concept of the healing crisis is an important one, meaning that in tackling such problems as guilt, resentment, or grief, you will at times stir up the very emotions you are trying to heal. Sometimes, as you honestly look at an area of life you'd like to change, the problem seems to flare up. Things aren't really getting worse, you've just removed your blinders and discovered how bad things got while you ignored the problem. Your consciousness has increased, not the difficulty. This reaction occurs with various types of therapy. A Pluto transit by itself is a healing crisis, even if you make no special efforts to work through the issues it raises.

Many of our "problems" are really attempts to keep our emotions at bay. In one of the Seth books by Jane Roberts listed in the bibliography, she says that all illness is an attempt to escape from the truth. In order to solve the problem, the emotions you are sitting on may need to come out. Thus, you may temporarily think things are getting worse while suppressed feelings come to the surface. If you've been sitting on anger about your mate's behavior for a long time, for example, a really big fight may be needed to clear the air and change the situation. (Please note that I am not advocating wholesale emoting all over the place without regard to others. There are mature ways of dealing with emotions without either suppression or harm to others.)

Both healing efforts and Pluto transits sometimes involve a temporary intensification of the struggle, almost as though the problem recognizes its hold on you is being threatened. It rises up as big and menacing as possible so you'll knuckle under again. The "IT" that is acting this way is not separate, but a part of your being which operates automatically. Developed as a legitimate means of survival under some earlier threat, this part persists and is inappropriately applied to new situations. Working with these parts is a technique developed by practitioners of NLP (Neuro-Linguistic Programming—see the bibliography for more information). As an experiment, you might try communicating with your Pluto part. For instance, you could sit down and write a letter which begins, "Dear Pluto," asking why you keep repeating a particular pattern. The answer could come as you write, or it might come in some other form, such as a dream.

I believe we all have a Higher Self (or soul) which guides us through life and which brings us particular experiences and people to further our development. Sometimes during a healing crisis (or a Pluto transit), this inner wisdom propels us into an extreme version of something we're trying to clear up. Let's say someone has Pluto in the sixth house and a pattern of feuding with coworkers, so under a particular transit he gets a new job with the meanest Plutonians of them all—the boss, secretary, and back-biting coworkers are Scorpios each and every one. He is definitely outclassed, and in the ensuing battle he has to learn a whole new way of operating— cleaning up his act in the process. This can also happen with friendships or love affairs, but we have to push ourselves into the ultimate lousy situation to get so sick and tired of it that we stop. This happens in healing crises all the time. It's no fun, but it is the beginning of change.

The healing crisis is important to keep in mind as you work with your own Plutonian difficulties. The tools we will be using may well bring up painful feelings and memories. For instance, in working on guilt, you may have to experience exactly how much guilt you carry around. Yet, experiencing it anew and seeing exactly where it comes from is part of letting it go, and the end result is that you are no longer burdened. You are not simply dragging up the past, you are doing it for a healing purpose and with tools. The pain is temporary—the healing permanent.

As you do the exercises that follow, feelings out of your past will often arise—anger, resentment, hurt—and you may try to attach them to something in the present. "It's not logical," you say to yourself, "to be so angry over something that happened so long ago." For instance, you may be furious, suddenly, at a lover who left you ten years ago, but you inappropriately put that anger onto your present lover, a family member, or a good friend. You may attribute the rage to something a present lover has done, so you can say you have cause for the anger—but not to that extreme. Be aware of this tendency to displace feelings and keep redirecting them to the proper target.

Also, don't try to rationalize the feelings away. "That's all in the past; it doesn't make sense to cry over it." Don't cover hurt feelings over with phony sweetness and light. Real forgiveness and acceptance will come later, as you work the healing tools through to completion, but not until you've fully allowed yourself to experience the rage or hurt. Drinking, overeating, smoking too much, or using drugs or tranquilizers will shut the process down or dull its impact, so avoid doing those things. By neither acting on the emotions impulsively nor doing anything to shut them down, you get through them faster and have a better opportunity to heal yourself.

Does transformation always have to involve a healing crisis? Probably not—your problems could drop away in an instant if you changed your consciousness. Pluto problems are deeply entrenched, somewhat obsessive, and often contain an element of the Scorpion's sting, so you may not relinquish them easily. Most of us don't pull our hands away from the fire until it burns us. Most of us won't stop what is making us sick until we are sick and tired of being sick and tired. But you *can* choose not to beat your head against the wall. And very often astrology can help you see the wall you're beating your head against, see that there are other ways to get around the wall. An astrology reading—or reading about yourself in this book—can be a healing crisis all its own.

Astrology and Metaphysics

A problem has to have an internal base of operation— Trouble doesn't start in the world. It starts first in the mind before it appears in the world. A mental state always precedes action.[5]

Metaphysics is the study of how we all create our own reality through thought patterns. Many Plutonians are magicians, in that they are especially gifted at manifesting things through their thoughts and beliefs. When their beliefs are negative, the things they manifest confirm their negativity. Given these tendencies, destructive and self-fulfilling predictions should be avoided. For example, if the client accepts an astrologer's belief that his Pluto transit is going to be hell, that's what it becomes, rather than being used as an opportunity to transform painful old patterns. To offset negativity, most Plutonians could benefit from a study of metaphysics. (A list of recommended books is included in the bibliography.) Groups such as Religious Science or Unity provide classes and services where you can work on negative belief systems and create a more positive reality for yourself.

---

[5] Raymond Charles Barker, *Barkerisms*, p. 28.

Many astrologers are studying metaphysics and incorporating this philosophy into their practice. It is especially useful in working with Plutonians, because it stops any conviction that our reality is created by Pluto, Neptune, or Saturn. An understanding of the ways people create their own realities can offset the powerlessness we often feel in the Pluto areas of our lives—that area where the infamous THEY often looms the largest. Using the chart to explore attitudes contributing to undesirable conditions related to our natal Pluto can be very helpful.

Healing Tools

Two of the tools for changing rigid thought patterns are visualizations and affirmations. We can adapt those tools to offset the negative thinking Plutonians suffer from, as well as the negativity all too often imparted by astrology books or astrologers. Affirmations are statements you repeat several times a day or whenever a negative thought comes up. They are always stated in the positive rather than the negative, for the statement "I will *not* do X," contains within it the thought, "I will do X," therefore reinforcing the old programming. Some people write affirmations on cards and read them at odd hours of the day, like when on hold on the telephone or standing in line. You may wish to design your own affirmations, for more specific help in your personal situation. As an example, here are affirmations designed for Plutonian traits discussed in Chapter Two.

AFFIRMATIONS FOR PLUTONIANS

I replace resentment with detachment and compassion.

I allow this situation to develop naturally for the good of all.

I let go and let God.

I let go of my past and trust in my future.

I open my heart and my life to the right people.

Visualizations are little plays in your mind where you imagine the situation working out the way you would like. It would be difficult to print visualizations here to suit your specific situation, but you can design them for yourself. For instance, let's say you are feeling resentful because the boss is always taking credit for your work. You might write affirmations that would help change this, such as "I receive credit and recognition for my contributions. My relationship with my employer is one of mutual respect." In addition, visualize yourself speaking to your boss about the unfairness of the situation, but handling it with consummate tact. Imagine him or her responding well and giving you credit at a staff meeting. It is not necessary that you "see" anything as you work with these mind plays. Simply imagining them is powerful enough.

FLOWER ESSENCES AND OTHER REMEDIES

The Bach Flower Remedies, California Flower Essences, and gem elixirs are homeopathic remedies for emotional and spiritual difficulties. They help with guilt, resentment, controllingness, and other long-standing personality patterns. Not a drug or a chemical, these liquid essences are highly diluted and natural. They work on subtle vibrational levels the way homeopathic preparations for physical conditions do. They cleanse the aura, mending the damage from years of emotional excesses and producing significant changes in behavior and well being. I have used them with astrology and therapy clients for more than four years, and I find real and lasting changes take place in only a few months.

If this sounds strange to you, the effectiveness of the flower essences has been demonstrated by a careful study, using rigorous modern research techniques. For his dissertation, Dr. Michael Weisglas gave preparations to three groups—one with a mixture of four remedies, one with seven remedies, and one with the same bottle of liquid but no remedies. Neither the people who took the remedies, nor the people who passed them out, knew who was getting which kind of bottle, so it was what is called a double blind study. Psychological tests were given beforehand, at three weeks, and at six weeks. People who got bottles with no remedies in them did not change, so it was not a matter of faith. For the others, the tests showed that the remedies deepened self-acceptance, enhanced personal growth, and increased well-being, creativity, humor, self-understanding, and sexual fulfillment.[6]

There are three main sets of remedies, although more are being developed. You may be able to find some in your area by looking in New Age newsletters or catalogues or by writing to the companies to ask for local practitioners. Failing that, the companies themselves mix remedies and send them by mail. Some health food stores sell either the concentrates or pre-mixed combinations by Deva. Books and sources of supplies are listed in the bibliography.

The oldest and longest tested are the Bach Flower Remedies. Developed in England in the 1930s during the Depression, they reflect the needs of that time, since they are for fear, depression, resentment and other intensely painful emotions and patterns. The more difficult problems Plutonians face seem to fit into the Bach kit. Remedies specific to the problems discussed in various chapters will be mentioned as we go along. Those general to the Plutonian are Willow, for resentment and bitterness, Vine, for the desire to control and dominate, Water Violet for the aloof person who does not care to mix in with ordinary people or their affairs, Chicory for possessive, martyr types who are constantly seeking to put others right, and Heather for lonely people who are wrapped up in their own problems. White Chestnut is for mental worries and obsessions.

The California Flower Essences were developed during the 1970s and also reflect their era, the height of the human potential movement. Thus, they have more to do with creativity, spiritual growth, and self-actualization. Some of the California Flower Essences address the painful problem of alienation and isolation: Dogwood is for receptivity to love, Shooting Star for feeling you don't belong in this world, Mariposa Lily for the feeling of separateness.[7] Both the Bach group and the California group publish newsletters and journals, and run training programs as well. The third major supplier,

---

[6] Michael Weisglas, Ph.D., "Bach Flower Essence Research: A Scientific Study," *The Flower Essence Journal*, v.1:1, 1980, pp. 11–14.

[7] In another book, *Flower Essences*, it is stated that Shooting Star is helpful for studying astrology. While this sounds contradictory, astrologers often do feel alienated and not of this world. (See *Flower Essences*, Gurudas, Brotherhood of Life, Albuquerque, NM, 1983, p. 186.)

Pegasus Products, has most of the same remedies as the other two groups plus many others. The Pegasus remedy Mallow is for help in making friends.

The remedies come in concentrated form, in a liquid. Two to four drops of each concentrate are put in one ounce of spring water, generally in an amber bottle something like those used for eyedrops. Shake the bottle well to mix all the concentrates together. Many people use a teaspoonful of brandy or of apple cider vinegar in the bottle as a preservative.[8]

It is best not to overdo it, probably using no more than four at one time. People who prescribe them consider it wise to test with a pendulum or muscle reflexology to see if this particular remedy is good at this time. You take four drops of the diluted version four times a day. Taking them in the morning, to set your frame of mind for the day, and the last thing at night, to work with the dreams, is a good practice. Although the research showed faith is not what makes the remedies work, using visualizations and affirmations with them seems to enhance the result.

Like all the tools we will discuss, the remedies can produce a temporary upsurge of the feelings they are designed to heal. The feelings don't get worse, you are just more aware of them and of the thought patterns behind them. Heightened awareness is part of the process—ultimately the thoughts sound so ridiculous and embarrassing that there is an impetus to change. The healing crisis seems to last only a few days. As you keep taking the remedy, it evens out. You might need to take two or more bottles of the mixture to change a long-ingrained habit but the day comes when you realize you are different, that a situation that once would have triggered resentment, guilt or obsessive thoughts has come up and you didn't react.

The remedies are an excellent tool for the astrologer. They are not difficult to learn and enable you to give the client something more than insight. Knowing what transits are going on helps pinpoint the most crucial areas to work on with the remedies, for transits produce

---

[8] Recovering alcoholics would obviously not want to use brandy. The concentrates themselves are preserved in brandy, so for alcoholics I reduce the formula to one drop of each concentrate, using the vinegar as a preservative. This doesn't seem to bring up the drink signals.

their own healing crisis as well as motivation to work on a particular difficulty. For instance, if you have Venus and Pluto in aspect, resentments over old loves may be getting in the way of finding a relationship. If a transiting planet forms an angle to Venus or Pluto, it would be an ideal time to take Willow, which is for resentment, and Honeysuckle, which is for letting go of the past. The California essence Bleeding Heart (for releasing painful emotional attachments) is also quite powerful. Or, suppose the chart suggests that suspiciousness and jealousy are threatening the person's marriage (another Pluto problem). Holly (for suspicion and jealousy) would be extremely helpful in changing this pattern.[9]

HEALING WITH LIGHT AND COLOR

In various books, whether psychological or occult, you can read about the properties of various colors. Even industry and designers are becoming aware of the effects of having various colors around us or wearing them. In books on color psychology, you read that blue works to mitigate fear or anxiety by making you more calm; red raises energy, courage, and assertiveness; pink softens and brings more loving feelings; and green stimulates health and financial well-being. The advent of Pluto in Scorpio has coincided with purple becoming a major fashion trend. . .almost a basic. Not too surprisingly, purple has to do with processing resentments, and it seems we as a people are drawn to purple now to heal our differences.

Healers work with color also, and sometimes with light, but not always on the physical level. More often, they work with the kind of light contained in the aura. By imagining purple, for instance, the higher consciousness of the individual is stimulated to begin releasing and processing old resentments. The meditations given in various places in this book make use of this kind of light. It is not necessary for you to see it for it to work—only a portion of people are visually inclined. Simply trust that the greater part of you, the Higher Self,

---

[9] I have recorded a tape entitled "Astrological Correlations to the Bach Flower Remedies" explaining the remedies and how to use them in astrological work with both natal charts and transits. It is available from RKM Enterprises, Box 23042, Euclid, OH 44123, for $7.95 plus $1.00 postage and handling.

knows how to create this kind of light. Working with light and color (whether by the clothes you wear or in your imagination) may bring on a healing crisis. It stimulates the release of stored up emotions, which can be uncomfortable but which is part of the healing process.

THE CHAKRAS AND THEIR HEALING IMPACT

Many spiritual traditions recognize the existence of the aura or energy body. Within it are energy organs, called centers or chakras, which regulate the intake and outflow of life force. Damming up this crucial energy often results from traumatic life situations, such as those shown by difficult Pluto placements or transits. For instance, damming up the heart center can create problems in giving and receiving love. An obstruction to the solar plexus can result in a need for excess attention or in poor self-esteem. The exercises in this section open up the flow of energy, and working with them is a powerful form of healing we all can do for ourselves.

The first center, the root chakra, is located at the base of the spine. Blockages could result in poor grounding and insecurity, with a constant focus on survival. Natally or by transit, Pluto aspects to the Moon, the fourth, or first house might result in uprooting or other traumas that could damage the root chakra. (We are focusing on Pluto here, but difficult aspects from other planets could create similar blockages in these centers.)

The second or sacral chakra governs reproduction and the flow of sexual energy; stress could result in under– or over–emphasis on sexuality, or in fears or resentments about one's gender. Different teachings give different locations for this center, some saying it is two inches below the navel, others saying that men have it in the area of the testicles. A strong Pluto in general, natal or transiting Pluto aspects to Mars or Venus, or difficult eighth house placements might create stress to this center through traumatic sexual experiences or difficulty in childbirth.

The third center is in the solar plexus area, just above the waist. This center rules self-expression and the self concept, and blockages could create low self esteem and a lack of self confidence, or its less obvious reverse, egotism, narcissism, and self-centeredness. It is related to the Sun in astrology, so Sun/Pluto aspects natally or by transit quite often create difficulty here, but Pluto/Saturn aspects could also lead to problems.

The fourth center is the heart chakra, located in the area of the actual physical heart. It is a crucial center regulating our ability to give and receive love, so blockages could create relationship problems and a sense of lack of loving exchange with the outer world. Natally or by transit, a Venus/Pluto aspect could cause problems here, but so could Pluto in the first house, since the person often has felt isolated and alone from an early age. Conversely, a symbiotic relationship with a parent could have demanded too much output from an immature heart center.

The fifth center, located in the throat, governs communication and other expressions of one's abilities, as well as dealing with money. Strong Pluto placements in general could dam up the throat center, but most especially a Mercury/Pluto aspect natally or by transit, or Pluto in the third house. The sixth or brow center, located between the eyes, has to do with mental clarity and intuitive communication. Blockages could create mental confusion or obsessiveness or difficulty in regulating psychic input. Again a Mercury/Pluto aspect might be implicated. The crown center is located at the top of the head and has to do with inspirational or meditative states, where one is in touch with the divine; blockages would lead to spiritual lows, losing that sense of connection with the Universe. Pluto in the twelfth or ninth house might cause this blockage.

The Whirlpool Cleanse for Chakras

1. Go into a deeper level of consciousness by using a particular meditative technique you may already know or simply by breathing deeply and counting to three over and over again.

2. Erect a protective bubble around yourself and fill it with a particular color of light, according to your intuition. White light is always a good choice, as it contains all the other colors. Imagine the chakras and locate them within your body.

3. Beginning with the root chakra, imagine a whirlpool or funnel of light positioned at that location within the bubble and pointed toward your body. Instruct the whirlpool to blaze up and consume any dark areas in its path. The light will spin as long as it needs to, as you move on to other centers. Here obstructions would come from problems about feeling grounded or from old traumas related to survival.

4. Go on to the sexual chakra and erect another whirlpool, which again blazes up and consumes obstacles. Here the intention would be to create a balanced and healthy outflowing of sexual energy.

5. When the areas below feel relatively clear, move to the solar plexus and start a whirlpool there. In this area, the light would blaze up and burn away obstructions to a healthy, realistic self-esteem, including ego wounds and feelings of incompetence.

6. Letting the previous whirlpools spin, move to the heart center and start one there. The heart center, being so crucial and vulnerable, can stand any amount of cleansing, as older and deeper heart wounds surface. Here the light would burn obstructions to loving and being loved.

7. Next, erect a whirlpool at the throat center, where it would burn away obstructions to communication and also to a free flow of money.

8. Next, do the brow center, which would relieve obstacles to the creative and psychic energy flow.

9. Finally, make a whirlpool at the crown, which would cleanse obstacles to meditation and inspiration.

10. Observe which of the centers still have their whirlpools spinning, as these may need special work. Blaze up the light brightly in those areas for a few moments before stopping them all and dissolving the bubble.

11. Repeat this exercise over a few days until the chakras seem clear. Later, repeat with colors given in various chapters of this book or as

your intuition guides you. Even when you've finished, repeat the cleansing periodically to avoid the buildup of emotional and psychic overloads in the course of daily living.

Opening the Heart Flower

This exercise can be adapted for use on any of the chakras, but it is given here for the heart center, which is such a major one for opening up to more loving relationships and for mending old hurts and losses. Many people have suffered damage to the heart center, especially when Pluto transited through Libra. When used to open other chakras, the affirmations would be designed for the center in question. It is important to open and cleanse all the centers, not concentrating on one exclusively, for this would create an imbalance.

1. Place yourself in a bubble. Imagine your heart center as a beautiful many-petalled flower, with the petals closed. A positive color for the flower would be bright pink, since that is the color of love.

2. Starting at the outside, open the petals, one by one. With each petal, affirm your willingness to give and receive love. You may do it by saying inwardly, "I am open to love," or whatever seems pleasing to you. Actually moving your hands through your energy field as if you were opening the petals greatly increases the effect.

3. Keep opening petals and opening petals and opening petals, repeating the affirmations as you do.

4. As you near the center, notice that the petals are glowing with pink light, warm to the touch.

5. When the center itself is open, the pink light radiates from it and pulsates outward past the edge of your bubble. Say to yourself, "This light from my heart is a beacon to those who would rightfully share love with me." Draw down pink light from your Higher Self to send outward.

This exercise is a powerful one. As you do it, you may at first find it somewhat difficult, as the pain you are carrying in your heart center may come up. Yet allowing it to come up, thawing out and releasing the grief, is an important part of the process of healing yourself. As you work with it over time, you will notice movement and energy in that part of your body. When someone you care for comes around, there will be an outward rush of energy from the heart that feels uplifting. This chakra is quite sensitive and may close down easily when someone around you is insensitive or does something to hurt you. It may also close down at times in self-protection. When it has closed, you will notice the absence of those heart rushes and know that it is time to work on the exercise again.

EASY DOES IT

As obsessive and compulsive as Plutonians are, once they find a tool to help them work through their difficulties they are likely to overdo it in their zeal to get better. It is important not to overwork these tools, as long-standing conditions need to heal more slowly. You would not want to be working on too many issues at one time, even though it is tempting to do so when you have finally found something that would help. A good rule is to only work on the meditations five days a week.

You can use several tools at once for greater effectiveness: for example, coordinating the flower remedy for resentment with the meditations for resentment, yet when you do so you could conceivably increase the magnitude of the healing crisis. If it becomes too intense, simply stop for a while. It is also a good rule to give yourself a complete rest from all healing efforts—for instance, stop the remedies altogether for six weeks every now and then.

These tools are exciting additions to the practice of astrology, and it is my hope that more astrologers will be attracted to healing work. Astrology is an unparalleled diagnostic tool, yet once you learn what the problems are, there is a great need to find ways to alleviate them. This chapter is only an introduction; the bibliography will suggest places to find out about these tools in greater depth.

Books About Flower Remedies

Bach, Edward, M.D. and F. J. Wheeler, M.D. *The Bach Flower Remedies*, Keats Health Books, New Canaan, CT, l979. (Published in the UK by C.W. Daniel, Ltd., Saffron, Walden.) The original descriptions of the remedies and their purposes by the man who developed them. Not as comprehensive or understandable as Chancellor's book, but considered the Bible on remedies.

Chancellor, Dr. Phillip M. *Handbook of the Bach Flower Remedies*, Keats Health Books, New Canaan, CT, 1971. (Published in the UK by C.W. Daniel Ltd., Saffron, Walden.) The best book about the Bach Flower Remedies. There is a description of each of the remedies with the purpose and personality traits it is designed to heal. There are case histories about each remedy, including the physical ailments of the person which cleared up as the emotional difficulties underlying them got better.

The Flower Essence Journal, Flower Essence Services, Box 586, Nevada City, CA 94939. Four large issues and periodic newsletters about continuing discovery of the meaning and uses of the flower essences, with contributions by people of various disciplines.

Gurudas. *Flower Essences*, Brotherhood of Life, 110 Dartmouth SE, Albuquerque, NM, 87106, l983. A book on the various flower essences which has quite interesting things to say about correspondences between the forms of plants and their healing purposes.

Gurudas. *Gem Elixirs and Vibrational Healing*. Casandra Press, Box 2044, Boulder, CO, 80306. Gem Elixirs and flower essence combinations and how these can be used to work on chakras and subtle bodies to heal disease.

Sources of Remedies, Books, and Supplies

Bach remedies: Ellon Company, Box 320, Woodmere, N.Y., 11598; and Bach Centre, Mount Vernon, Sotwell, Oxon, UK.

California remedies: Flower Essence Services, Box 586, Nevada City, CA 94939

Pegasus: Pegasus Products Inc., Box 228, Boulder, CO 80306

Metaphysical Books

Gawain, Shakti. *Creative Visualization*, Whatever Publishing, Mill Valley, CA, 1978. One of the better how-to books on using visualizations and affirmations to help yourself.

Roberts, Jane. *The Nature of Personal Reality*, Prentice-Hall, Englewood Cliffs, N.J., 1974. The most profound exposition of metaphysics available; much slower going than the pop metaphysics books, yet full of important, powerful material about the way our personal reality is shaped by our thoughts. One of a series of books channeled by the medium Jane Roberts through the being Seth.

Other Healing Topics

Bandler, Richard, and John Grinder. *Frogs Into Princes*, Real People Press, Box F, Moab, UT, 84532, 1979. The basic book about Neuro-Linguistic Programming, a fast-acting therapeutic method distilled from the work of the greatest therapists of our time and incorporating some of the principles of hypnosis and linguistics. Part of a series of teaching works on this method, including the excellent *Trance-Formations*, same authors and press, 1981.

Clark, Linda. *The Ancient Art of Color Therapy*, Pocket Books, N.Y., 1975. An excellent paperback on the healing art of color therapy as practiced in other countries. It focuses more on the physical and emotional effects of actual light and color, rather than the auric colors we are working with here; however the two methods can reinforce one another.

Wallace, Amy and Bill Henkin. *The Psychic Healing Book*, Wingbow Press, Berkeley, CA, 1981. A simply written guidebook for learning about psychic healing and about grounding and shielding techniques. Sensible, down-to-earth, not spooky in any way. The best guide of its kind, very accessible.

CHAPTER FOUR

Guilt, Resentment, and Pluto

Guilt and resentment are so intimately related that you might call them Siamese twins—you can't have one without the other. If either guilt or resentment makes your life difficult, this chapter will help you understand what creates them and what you can do to get rid of them through considering the dynamics of the planet Pluto. We will find the familiar patterns of symbiosis, control, vengefulness, and holding on. The final section of this chapter contains exercises and suggestions for ridding yourself of guilt and resentment.

All of us have Pluto and Scorpio somewhere in our charts, and all of us have suffered these painful, alienating emotions. The sick, tummy-twisting feeling of guilt or the burning, obsessive, brooding feeling of resentment are all too familiar to most of us. Resentment alienates us from our fellow man, while guilt alienates us from ourselves. Plutonians are tormented by these feelings, which lock them into rigid defenses and dominate relationships. Let's look at the connections between guilt and resentment, so you can understand and overcome them. In order to get the most of this information, take a minute to make a list of the situations where you personally feel guilty or of people you feel guilty toward.

Don't Be Beguiled by Guilt

Of the Siamese twins, guilt and resentment, let's begin with guilt. The truth is, guilt is a crock. The words guile and guilt have the same root, and there is a great deal of guile involved. People who try to make you feel guilty are being deceptive about their motives. Behind the high-sounding protestations of love and concern, the real desire is to manipulate you so that you do what they want. "If you loved me, you'd. . ." This is emotional blackmail masquerading as love. Guilt works, though—it will make you fall in line faster than threats and overt domination. Guilt is about control. **A guilt trip is a power trip.** Anytime you feel swamped by guilt, ask yourself, is this person trying to manipulate me?

Guilt often arises where people are joined in the the false dependency we call symbiosis—which is like being joined at the hip—a Pluto pattern. Most of the time, people who do too much for us or give too much to us don't do it out of the sheer goodness of their hearts. They do it because they want to call the shots. Is it really goodness to rob someone of the opportunity to learn and grow into greater independence? Is it goodness to make you believe you're incompetent to make a move without them? At some level, you know you're being robbed, and you come to resent the symbiosis. When you assert yourself or "selfishly" want to do what you need for your own happiness and further development, your so-called benefactor pulls the strings to manipulate you into feeling guilty. Again, the Plutonian motive is control. It's all very subtle, of course, and that's why it's so effective.

Yes, the guilt trip is a power trip, and guilt is guile. But you can't con an honest man, and a guileless man knows no guilt. In other words, you are covering something up when you fall for a guilt trip, like bogus dependency and unwillingness to take responsibility for yourself, so that you've given over the power to the Plutonian. You're conning the Plutonian into being your Mommy. Ask yourself if the reward is worth the price in self-esteem and growth. In the end, no matter how long you delay, you still have to take responsibility.

The other way you're conning yourself (and other people) is that your guilt trip is *also* a power trip. You are clinging to the illusion that your actions have so much power that you are indispensable to their happiness. The truth is, we are immortal and indestructible, so short of murder or mayhem, none of our actions have that much power to harm anyone else, except if they are playing Pluto games of their own.

If honestly going after your own development makes the other person that unhappy, then there is a false dependency. In a situation like that, going your own way so that you can grow in independence doesn't harm the other person, it forces him or her to grow as well, so you may be doing a favor in the end. If you allow yourself to be manipulated by guilt into stifling your own growth, you will begin to resent the person who manipulates you.

There is another sense in which guilt is conning yourself. One psychologist whose name escapes me said that guilt is the price we are willing to pay for holding onto a false self-concept while continuing to violate it. Wherever there is a SHOULD, suspect that this kind of false self-image may be operating. Where you have expectations of perfection or saintliness for yourself, there are two ways to get rid of guilt: change your behavior, or change your expectations. Guilt that you hang on to is license to keep doing wrong, to keep conning yourself and others into thinking you are trying to improve.

Guilt Is Resentment Turned Inward

Since the development of a guilt-laden character structure arises from abandonment of the effort to develop mature independence, it represents a retreat into infantile dependency. . .This produces vague moods of resentment as well as a general sense of guilt.[10]

Most of us are familiar with the psychological teaching that depression is anger turned inward. Very few people, however, know that guilt is resentment turned inward. As small children, adults seem all-powerful over our very survival. When they try to correct us, when they try to keep us under control, we resent it, but there is very little we can do. They have so much power and we have so little. The resentment turns inward and changes into a feeling we label guilt.

---

[10] Sue Mansfield, *The Gestalt of War*, Dial Press, NY, 1982, p. 101.

Even as adults, we retain some of that childlike dependency. No one is ever entirely grown up, so none of us can escape guilt and resentment, but the most guilt-laden people are those who have retreated most into inappropriate dependency. Wherever guilt exists, there also exists an abuse of power. When we get involved with power-tripping Plutonian people, feelings of powerlessness are activated by their manipulations. We become symbiotically dependent, and when they try to control us, the ensuing resentment is perceived as guilt. "How can I be angry at her when she is so good to me? I feel so guilty. She knows what's best for me." Sheldon Kopp says that guilt is no more than the secret resentment of unwanted obligations.[11]

Now, you may have done some terrible things. You're not a saint, and probably you've done a few nasties. But sometimes such actions are self-defense. Unerringly, you do the very thing they can't bear, the unkindest cut of all, a betrayal of trust. Chances are, you did it as a way of ending the relationship or evening the score. There was no other way of cutting through the game that was going on in the relationship, no other way out.

At times, guilt is no more than a vengeful ploy in a power struggle. It's a con game, like Lucy Brown in the Peanuts comic strip swearing over and over that she's sorry for jerking the football away from her brother, that she'll never do it again. Then she sets him up to kick the football just this one more time, only to pull it away at the last minute so he'll fall flat on his face again. Oh, I know that rotten Lucy has no conscience, whereas you feel guilty, but that's only the price of admission to the game. By beating your breast with self-loathing, buying a bunch of flowers, and begging for forgiveness, you've invalidated their anger and set them up so you can shaft them all over again. For that kind of guilt, you should feel guilty.

Behavior like this often comes out of the Plutonian desire for revenge. Perhaps the people you keep doing these things to made you excessively dependent and you are trying to strike back. Or, perhaps you are acting out resentment toward a parent or other authority figure. Unfortunately, vengefulness doesn't care who it strikes (the scorpion is a mindless creature), so you keep making all women or all

---

[11] Sheldon Kopp, *The Hanged Man*, Science and Behavior Books, Palo Alto, CA, 1974, p. 111.

men pay for what your mother or father did twenty or thirty years ago. But it's not nice to act that way, so you pay for it by guilt. Suffer enough guilt and you get a free ticket to do it again.

Getting caught is another useful ploy in this particular game. Revenge isn't any fun if nobody knows about it. Getting caught is a real kick in the teeth, though, for the person you're getting revenge on. You get your revenge, at the cost of the consequences you have to pay (the scorpion's sting) and at the cost of guilt and self-loathing. But you still get your revenge. In the more morbid versions of the game, that's all that counts.

The Litmus Test for Guilt

You may wish to refer to the list you created earlier of people and situations where you feel guilty, or you may wish to take time now to make such a list. Considering all the things we've said, there are several questions to ask yourself when you have an attack of guilt:

- Am I involved in a symbiotic and false dependency?
- Am I abdicating responsibility for my own life?
- Are they laying a power trip on me?
- Am I doing a power trip or con job of my own?
- Are they limiting my growth or vice versa by guilt?
- What in this situation am I resenting?
- Am I using my guilt as license to keep on doing it?
- Am I trying to get even with this person?
- Am I trying to get even with the parent this person represents?

Once you have answered these questions, you will have a better understanding of the situation. By seeing it more clearly, you will have an idea of whether there is, in fact, anything to feel guilty about. If the action you feel guilty about contributed to your growth, it was probably right for you to do it. Perhaps you didn't do it in a kind or considerate way, and you may need to make amends for that. You can never make another person happy by stifling your own development, however, because that inevitably leads to resentment, usually on the part of both you and the individual involved.

The Existential Guilt of the Plutonian

What you will not find on your list is the guilt that preceded it—guilt waiting for a transgression or even an anticipated transgression to fasten onto. You walk around with it eating at you, and since no one likes to feel guilty without a reason, you invent one. "I shouldn't have spoken so sharply to her. I should have called to see how she was doing. I should have tried harder. I must be a scum bag to have such disloyal thoughts. As a matter of fact, I AM a scum bag; I can't imagine why anyone likes me. They wouldn't if they really knew how I am."

I call this existential guilt. If you have it, you had it long before you were old enough to do any real harm to anyone. Freudians would say it has to do with toilet training. I say it has to do with the toilet trainers and with the resentment they had about taking care of a baby. Such children pick up the fact that Mommy doesn't seem to like them, at least when they are hungry or tired or sick, so the children conclude it's bad to have needs and that they are unlovable. They come to have guilt about taking up space on the planet, about needing anything, about existing at all. And, underneath it and feeding it, there is also resentment about not being loved and nurtured rightly.

People may do one of two things with existential guilt. One is to spend your life in atonement, being as saintly as you can and dedicating your life to serving others. (And secretly being *very* angry, so that it permeates the atmosphere around you.) Or, rather than becoming a saint, you might become a sinner, finding transgressions to account for the guilt and punishments to atone for it. This is also a way of getting even with your parents, blackening their good name.

How do I know about existential guilt? I had it. I used to have it so bad that when a police car went by I would cringe. I'd never done anything illegal in my life, but somehow I was convinced they were going to arrest me and take me away. I got over it by the processes outlined in this chapter, and by now anyone would be hard put to manipulate me through guilt. It is beautiful to be free of it.

When Is Guilt Justified and Helpful?

Sheldon Kopp says, "I believe we are not punished FOR our sins, but BY them."[12] By now, you may be asking if there is ever a reason to feel guilty. Yes, I do believe that there are times when guilt is appropriate. Appropriate guilt arises when you abuse your own power. When you have been controlling, conning or manipulating someone for your own ends and not for his or her growth, you are abusing your power. There is also legitimate guilt when you are not doing your best to master yourself and grow spiritually. But legitimate guilt should never last more than a few minutes. Becoming aware that you have done wrong should be an occasion for growth, an uplifting of consciousness that says, "I won't do that again." It could be followed by a sincere attempt to make amends—not a sleazy "I'll make it up to you somehow," followed by repetition after repetition.

Like all manifestations of Pluto, the true purpose of guilt is *transformation*. If you don't hold onto guilt, but work through it, those moments of knowing you haven't done your best can strengthen your character and integrity, helping you function in the world in a more conscious, loving way. But that kind of good, wholesome guilt only comes when you've healed yourself of resentment. Thus, it is time to look at resentment and the part it plays in this nexus of difficult emotions.

Symbiosis, Power, and Resentment

In order to get the most out of this section, you may wish to take a few moments to make a list of the people you resent, the ones you hate, or the ones you never can forgive. Odd, isn't it, how many of those same people appeared on your guilt list? By now, it should be

---

[12] Kopp, *The Hanged Man*, p. 216.

getting clear that the people we resent most are people we depend on most. Outsiders may make us angry by thoughtless actions, but only those who have real or imagined power over us can make us resentful. We hold anger in because we are afraid of desertion or retaliation. The more false dependency on the person, the more we have abdicated our own power, the more afraid we are to show our anger. We are afraid we'll lose their seemingly indispensable help.

It should be said that both partners in the symbiotic relationship are Plutonian, in that both are trying to manipulate and control the other in order to sustain the symbiosis. The "mommy" is dependent on the "child's" dependency in order to feel powerful and in control. Yet, when we try to control something, it winds up controlling us. Control takes a tremendous amount of energy and never works for very long.

Such a stifling relationship readily generates a two-way resentment. The overtly dependent person comes to resent the inequality and the loss of growth and freedom. The overtly giving person comes to resent having to give so much. *The gift not willingly given is no gift at all*. In fact, any time you resent having to give something, suspect that a Plutonian dynamic is going on, where you fear that not giving will mean you are going to be abandoned. Since the "giving" makes the receiver more and more dependent, both people can become increasingly resentful, leading to the kinds of nasties we talked about under guilt. Ultimately, escalating resentment can lead to a bitter and painful parting that may haunt each person for years.

The truth is, real intimacy—Venus intimacy, not Pluto—is impossible without equality and the freedom to express and resolve conflicts that naturally arise in any relationship. Anger that is held in ferments and creates distance. If you consistently do something which annoys me but I am afraid to tell you, the unspoken anger grows and eventually pollutes the relationship. Only by open discussion of the conflict, as two equal partners, can the relationship grow. When the relationship is unequal, the anger is more likely to be held in out of fear and it eventually changes into resentment. When enough resentment is stored up, the relationship is destroyed and the feared abandonment actually happens.

Sometimes we carry resentments around for years after these painful partings. This is also an illusory power trip—a way of holding on to other people, even though they may have long since forgotten us. We fantasize about meeting them again—or "dread" another meeting. We fantasize getting even. We fantasize getting rich and powerful—or dead—just to show them or to make them sorry they ever left us. The very folks we love to hate are usually the ones we once loved the most. It doesn't give us power over them, but it gives them immense power over us. In hanging onto the resentment long after the relationship has ended, we are *still* giving over power to the other person. The more we resent someone or something, the more power we give up, and the more we are controlled. These people become immensely important in our lives, even though we may now be insignificant in theirs. As we brood over them, they grow in our imagination, becoming less and less the real people we loved and more and more bigger-than-life monsters. Go visit the dragon; you may find nothing but a worm.

Resentment As Poison

A member of my healing group for alcoholics once asked, "What's the difference between anger and resentment? Aren't they the same?" (They aren't the same in astrology—anger is Mars and resentment is Pluto.) I replied that anger and resentment are the same only in the sense that grape juice and wine are. They start out the same, but resentment is anger that is fermented and aged like wine, thus becoming a more poisonous substance. The liver, on the spiritual level, metabolizes anger, and nobody ever got cirrhosis from grape juice.

Resentment is an enormous problem for the alcoholics I work with, so it is a factor in addiction and other tormenting patterns. It is also a poison to the body, causing problems like gallstones ("What she does galls me") and cancer, in which the things that are eating you up start eating away at your body. Conversely, a study has shown that cancer patients who are able to mobilize their anger have the best chance of surviving.[13]

---

[13] From a study by Sandra Levy of the University of Pittsburg Medical School, cited in *USA Today*, August 29, 1984, p. 1 in the article "Angry Patients Give Cancer Best Fight."

One of the side-effects of resentment is self-hate. It is as though our bodies were vessels, and when the vessels are filled with resentment that has no place to go, it backs up on us. Hatred of others becomes self-hate. The more self-hate we have, the more we are likely to form symbiotic "love" relationships of the Plutonian sort to try to reclaim our self-esteem through the other. Yet, self-esteem can't really come from anyone outside ourselves, and if we hate ourselves or others, we have a very hard time finding love.

The Plutonian who is motivated to get self-love through power over others rarely finds love, only hate. When you walk around resentful, your attitude alienates others. If you walk around with a chip on your shoulder, you find plenty of people who enjoy knocking it off. You become unhappy with your life because your relationships are so bad, and you come to blame God for your troubles. Progressively bitter alienation from God and man is the life history of many people with a strong Pluto.

The Pitfalls of Revenge and Spite

> *Vengeful people submerge grief in anger. . .They are unwilling or unable to accept that they are the sort of person to suffer injury. Revenge is an attempt to sustain an essentially false image of oneself.*[14]

Doubtlessly, revenge is an unpopular word for moderns. We talk about getting even, or getting back at someone. The phrase, "to get even," suggests there is an imbalance of power. If we have to get even, that means things were UNeven to begin with. If we didn't feel intimidated about asserting ourselves, we'd be able to do something, and we wouldn't wind up nursing a grudge. *Nursing* is a dependency word, and we resent most the very people we are most dependent on. The greatest and most sustained resentments leave us with a desire for revenge.

---

[14] Mansfield, *The Gestalt of War*, p. 50.

Often, when we are powerless and dependent in a relationship and have no direct way of striking back, we do things to ourselves out of spite. Children often do this, but many adults also do spiteful things to themselves to get back at their parents for things parents did long ago. For instance: a parent keeps telling the child he'll never amount to anything, so as an adult, he gets fired from one job after another. Or, a mother keeps telling a daughter she's fat and ugly; the girl gains more weight out of spite. When you say, "I'll show them," you generally show them by harming yourself. I call the house Pluto is in the *fail for spite* house. (See Chapter One.)

In addition, as Theodore Isaac Rubin points out, the search for vindictive triumph destroys our satisfaction in other important aspects of life, being unrelenting in its demands. He says, "The quest for vengeance puts our own drive and power outside ourselves, giving the person we must get even with power over us. . .It tends to push other, more important areas of our lives to the side."[15]

Both Plutonians and the sign Scorpio are known for vengefulness, and when the scorpion stings it kills not only its enemy but itself. All revenge is like that; the desire for it almost always poisons your consciousness, and acting on the desire for revenge often leads to a destructive escalation of the conflict. Most forms of vengeance are extremely Plutonian. Suicide is often a vengeful act. Telling the deep dark secret can often be done in a vengeful way, a la Christina Crawford.[16]

The major problem with revenge is that, as long as you go after it, you are controlled by it, and waste energy you could use to do something positive for yourself. You are mired in the past and cannot freely move toward the future. Thus, the work on letting go of resentments and forgiving is not for the sake of the other person but for YOURSELF. If need be, you can adopt the Scorpio version of the Lord's Prayer: "Forgive us our debts as we forgive our debtors, even though the bastards don't deserve it!"

---

[15] Theodore Isaac Rubin, MD, *Reconciliation: Inner Peace in an Age of Anxiety*, Viking Press, NY, 1980.

[16] According to her book, *Mommie Dearest*, Christina was born June 11, 1939, in the afternoon. This chart shows a t-square of Mars, Pluto, and Saturn, a combination indicating both abuse and deep anger about it.

Healing Tools:
How to Get Free of Resentment and Guilt

If you identify with the dynamics described here, what can you do? Pluto has its positive side too, and you can uplevel the energy of this planet from destructive to constructive. Pluto rules psychology and self-analysis, so you can purge yourself of the past by looking deep within and confronting yourself honestly. Pluto is the planet of rebirth, of healing and transformation. You can claim a new life for yourself, a joyful freedom from guilt and resentment, if you direct attention to recognizing and changing these patterns.

Healing begins with consciousness; the more awareness you have of the mechanisms behind guilt and resentment, the less likely you are to fall into them. At first the awareness can be painful, like a light suddenly turned on in the dark. As you adjust to seeing things in the new light, you'll prefer that to stumbling over them in the darkness. The second crucial step is to stop projecting the blame onto THEM. Except as children, or unless you were the victim of violence, if you were a victim, you contributed to the situation by abdicating your power, refusing to take full responsibility for yourself. Wayne Dyer's book, *Pulling Your Own Strings*, contributes insight into victim situations and help in getting out of them.[17]

Exploring guilt and resentment situations by writing or talking them out on tape can help you see them more clearly. Look at your lists of the people in your life you have deeply resented or the ones you feel guilty toward. Think them through in more depth, paying particular attention to situations in childhood and adolescence. Write about each one separately in more detail, considering the questions of power and dependency. Consider how your actions and character flaws played into the situation. For instance, did you make excessive demands for attention or nurturing, or fail to assert yourself or communicate about conflict? Did you let pride, fear, or infantile needs get in the way of an open, equal, sharing exchange? Consider, also, how symbiotic dependency applies to you in that relationship.

As an experiment, pretend to be the other person and write or talk out the incident from his or her point of view. How did your own

---

[17] Published by Avon, NY, 1977.

behavior look? What were the pressures, or what motives did the other person have? Does the situation look different when you see it in the light of these questions? The very act of thinking the lists through is healing, because seeing old situations in a new light will enable you to let go of some.

Listing the people you feel guilty towards is helpful in other ways. It establishes the boundaries of your guilt, so that it is specific rather than limitless. You can then decide whether your guilt was real and merited, or whether it arose out of a power trip. Even in some situations where you more or less deliberately hurt someone, you might consider whether or not the desire to hurt came out of resentment of power and dependency dynamics within the relationship.

There are situations where guilt is appropriate, and in those situations you may be able to relieve your guilt by making suitable amends to the person. If it is hard to think about making amends, you might wish to consider whether you also have a resentment toward that person which could be getting in the way. If so, you would first want to work on the resentment.[18]

In some instances, making amends can cause more harm than good—let's say you feel guilty because you were secretly unfaithful to your mate. A confession would do needless damage. Or, let's say you've embezzled money from your company and confession would mean losing your job, causing severe financial hardship for your family. You might also want to consider your motivation for confession in those circumstances to see if it is not a form of revenge. For those guilty secrets, the old ritual of confession served a valid healing purpose. If you can't go to confession (and you don't have to be a Catholic to avail yourself of that service), find a safe confessor elsewhere. Astrologers also take a vow of silence, so you might want to talk to one who is able to hear you. Not all astrologers are good counselors, but astrological counseling by a humanistically-inclined practitioner can be very healing. Plutonians isolate themselves by

---

[18] Chapters 8 and 9 of the Alcoholics Anonymous guidebook, *Twelve Steps and Twelve Traditions* (published by Alcoholics Anonymous World Services, Inc., Box 459, New York, NY 10017) gives you a process for relieving yourself of guilt and making amends to people you have harmed. You can find this book at your local library.

their guilty secrets and the isolation harms them. You are only as sick as your secrets.

FLOWER REMEDIES

In addition to these processes, there are also specific healing tools for guilt and resentment—guided meditations and flower essences. These tools were outlined in Chapter Three. Among the Bach flower remedies, Pine is the specific remedy for guilt. In addition, Crab Apple is for self-loathing and the feeling that you are somehow unclean. Sunflower, among the California essences, helps with balancing out the ego and restoring self-esteem. Fuschia and Scarlet Monkeyflower from the California kit also help with integrating powerful emotions and so could be helpful. For both guilt and resentment, the Bach remedy Honeysuckle is good, because it deals with letting go of the past, and both these emotions keep your energy stuck in the past.

For resentment, the Bach remedy Willow helps with bitterness, resentment, and the feeling that you've been given a raw deal. Holly is for hatred, jealousy, suspicion, and the desire for revenge—all those Plutonian goodies. If you are troubled with any of these, Holly would be a priority, because these emotions are exceedingly toxic ones which can poison all attempts at self-help. When resentment comes up as a result of a desire to control, Vine is the Bach remedy.

AFFIRMATIONS FOR GUILT

The past is meaningful only for what I can learn from it.

I regard myself and my past with loving compassion.

I accept responsibility for _____.

I find a way to make amends to _____, or if it would be harmful to do so, I let it go.

I trust in my ability to do better.

I forgive myself for all past transgressions.

GUIDED MEDITATIONS

The following meditations are designed to help you work through situations where guilt and resentment are troubling you—the ones on your list which haven't been totally relieved by the process we have been doing. You might find it helpful to read the steps out loud slowly onto a tape recorder, so you don't have to look at the book while you work. If you have any of the flower remedies discussed in the last section, it is quite powerful to take a drop of the relevant one in a glass of water as you begin the meditation.

AN EXERCISE FOR CLEANSING YOURSELF OF GUILT

You may wish to do the following exercise several times for each person on your list. It is particularly crucial to do it for your parents and mate.

1. Go down into a deep state of consciousness or pretend to. Ask your Higher Self for help in getting free of guilt.

2. Create a bubble of lovely, shimmering lavender light around yourself. Imagine your body as an empty outline, and fill that in with a lavender fire.

3. Some distance outside yourself, create another bubble of lavender light, and inside it place the person or situation you feel guilty toward. Create them in as much detail as possible, replaying the events and allowing the guilt feelings to rise.

4. Imagine that the other bubble becomes a powerful magnet, drawing out of your body the guilt you have stored up there. Go deeper into consciousness if you need to. Call on your Higher Self for help in releasing the situation.

5. When you have released as much as you can, shift the bubble around behind you to draw out unconscious or forgotten guilt feelings or those you have taken in psychically from that person. You may notice that it is even more powerful from the back.

6. When you have done as much of that as you can, move the bubble back in front of you. Look at the person or situation again. If he or she does not seem changed to you, shrink that bubble in size to reduce the person's power over you.

7. Blaze the other person's bubble up as a lavender fire that blots out the picture and burns away the residue of guilty feelings. When the fire is a clear, iridescent lavender, burst the bubble and disperse the light into the atmosphere.

8. Blaze the fire up in your own bubble, asking your Higher Self to remove any remaining paralyzing guilt and to give you clarity on any action you should take to make amends.

9. Let go of the lavender light, replacing it with white. Come back up to your normal waking consciousness.

10. Repeat the exercise periodically, on all the people on your list, until you are free of needless guilt.

Working this exercise through to completion brings a heady, joyful feeling and changes your relationships for the better. For one thing, it will be harder for people to control you! It also helps your self-esteem immensely.

AFFIRMATIONS FOR RESENTMENT

I reclaim my own power in this situation.

I assert myself effectively and appropriately.

I accept responsibility for my part in the conflict.

I accept with serenity those situations I cannot change.

I am willing to forgive _____ for his/her actions.

Bless and release _____ to his/her higher good.

AN EXERCISE FOR CLEANSING YOURSELF OF RESENTMENT

You may wish to do the following exercise several times for each person on your resentment list. It is particularly crucial to do it for your parents and mate.

1. Go down into a deep state of consciousness or pretend to. Ask your Higher Self for help in letting go of resentments.

2. Create around yourself a bubble of rich, deep purple light, something like sunshine glowing through a purple stained glass window. Imagine your body as an empty outline, and fill that in with a purple fire.

3. Some distance outside yourself, create another bubble of purple light, and inside it place the person or situation you have resentment about. Imagine the person in as much detail as possible, replaying the events vividly and allowing resentment to rise to the surface.

4. Imagine that the other bubble becomes a powerful magnet, drawing out of your body the resentment you have stored. Go deeper into consciousness if you need to. Call on your Higher Self for help in releasing it.

5. When you have released as much as you can, shift the bubble around behind you to draw out unconscious or forgotten resentments. You may notice that it is even more powerful from the back.

6. When you have done as much as you can, move the bubble back in front of you. Look at the person or situation again. If he or she does not seem changed, shrink that bubble to reduce the person's power over you.

7. Blaze the person's bubble up as a purple fire that blots out the picture and burns away the residue of the resentment. Send the ball deeply into the ground, near the center of the earth.

8. Blaze the purple fire up in your own bubble, asking your Higher Self to remove any remaining resentment.

9. Let go of the purple light, replacing it with white. Come back up to your normal waking consciousness.

10. Repeat the exercise periodically, on all the people on your list, until you are free of resentment.

AN EXERCISE FOR LETTING GO

If you are still having difficulty letting go of a person or situation, the exercise which follows is quite helpful:

1. Put yourself in a bubble of white light and go down deep into consciousness. Connect with your Higher Self and express your desire and intention to be free of this person or situation.

2. Imagine that you are on the bank of a large, powerful river. A small boat is tied up there, and the strong current tugs on the boat, ready to sweep it downstream.

3. Imagine the person in as much detail as possible. Recognize that he or she has a Higher Self also, which is totally separate from yours. Speak through your Higher Self to the Higher Self of the other, explaining that you need to be free of the negative bond that is tying the two of you together.

4. Now pick up a big, sharp knife that is lying there and use it to cut through the rope that ties the boat to the dock. Hold on to the end of the rope.

5. Hold the rope in your hand, and tell the person through his or her Higher Self, "I hereby voluntarily release you. Go on your own path to good."

6. Let go of the rope, and watch as the current swiftly carries the boat and the person downstream. Say goodbye to it as it gets smaller and smaller. Wish it well. Know that the river can't reverse itself and go back upstream, so the boat is gone for good and you have relinquished your hold on that person or thing.

7. Mourn if you need to, but know that better things are coming in its place. You haven't lost the good that came from the situation, only the pain.

Forgiveness as the Greatest Healing

Doing the previous exercises to completion should bring you a long way toward freedom from resentment, hate, and bitterness toward people and situations in your past and present. These poisonous emotions steal your energy and vitality—heavy burdens which keep you from living joyfully and richly. Your ill will toward someone else, whether conscious or unconscious, boomerangs back on you emotionally and spiritually. It cuts you off not only from the person you have come to hate (who no doubt you once loved), but from a loving exchange with others around you who sense the hate in you and are put off by it. Finally, it cuts you off from a free flow of sustaining energy from spiritual sources, who are pushed away by negative energy.

We have explored the ways resentment poisons your life. To be healed, you must become willing to forgive. This may sound outrageous, it may even sound impossible, but it is the only way to get free of resentment. Forgiveness is a necessity for your own healing rather than out of any goody-goody impulse toward the other person. A powerful book teaching the steps we go through in order to forgive is Doris Donnelly's *Learning to Forgive*. As Donnelly says, "When I am hurt, physically or spiritually, my wounds have power over me, they tell me what I can or can't do. . . .Forgiveness is a power that serves as an antidote to the energy of the pain that directs me."[19] Donnelly does not recommend a phony, sweetness-and-light forgiveness. She describes a profound experience in which the resentment

---

[19] Doris Donnelly, *Learning to Forgive*, Festival Books Edition, Abingdon Press, Nashville, TN, 1980, p. 72.

and hurt must first be fully experienced. I would heartily recommend this book to those whose lives are darkened by resentment. It seems to me that forgiveness and reconciliation of our differences with others can be the end point of Pluto in Scorpio. We will first bring out the secrets, the long-standing grudges, the unspoken hatreds, and work with them until we are through them, so we will all be happier and freer.

AN EXERCISE FOR FORGIVENESS

1. Put yourself in the bubble of white light. Reach up for your Higher Self and ask for help in getting free of this burden.

2. Now create a second bubble of light and put the person you are working on forgiving into it. Imagine this person in as much detail as possible, particularly as he or she was when the difficulty arose. It would also help to ask the person's Higher Self to work with you in releasing you both from this negative bond.

3. Imagine yourself swimming backwards in the river of time to the period when this was going on. Recreate the scene in as much detail as possible, recapturing the emotions you felt.

4. Let the emotions well up until they fill your bubble. Then imagine that a warm golden rain washes them out of the bottom of the bubble until they are all gone.

5. Once more calling on your Higher Self as well as the other person's, imagine a revolving door between your bubbles. Step into it, while the other person steps into the other side, and use the revolving door to exchange places.

6. Go down deeply into consciousness, and experience the other person's feelings about the situation. Explore that period from his or her point of view, particularly what pressures and needs were operating.

7. Play the scene out once more from the other person's point of view. How does it feel? How does the person experience *your* behavior?

8. Now step back into the revolving door, and have the other person do the same. Make the turn back into your own bubble, and contemplate what you learned about the situation. Calling on your Higher Self once again, ask for the willingness to let go of the situation. Come back up to waking consciousness.

9. Repeat the exercise periodically until you are able to let go.

Isn't It Worth the Effort?

Guilt and resentment are painful and persistent emotions. They bind your energy up in the past, handicapping you for living effectively in the present. Clearing out these patterns is like suddenly losing forty unwanted pounds. You feel lighter, freer, and more a part of the human race. Loving exchanges with others become more and more frequent. Yes, there is temporary pain in confronting your part in these situations, but it is nothing compared to your future joy. Work the processes described here honestly and thoroughly and you will get free. If enough of us do work like this during Pluto in Scorpio, tons of dynamite in the form of hate and self-hate can be removed for the greater good of all of us.

Books to Heal Guilt and Resentment

Donnelly, Doris. *Learning to Forgive*. Festival Books Edition, Abingdon Press, Nashville, TN, 1980. An excellent work on the necessity for forgiveness and the healing process that makes it possible. Written from a religious framework, yet not denying the pain and anger. (Sometimes found in religious bookstores.)

Dyer, Wayne. *Pulling Your Own Strings*. Avon, N.Y., 1977. A useful book that contributes insight into your victim situations and helps you get out of them. When you do not feel trapped into being a victim, you build up less resentment.

Rubin, Theodore Isaac, M.D. *Compassion and Self-Hate*. Ballantine, N.Y., 1975. A healing book on the roots of our guilt and self-hate, one with transformative effects.

_____. *The Angry Book*. Macmillan, N.Y., 1979. Another of Rubin's many excellent self-help works, this one focusing on anger and the consequences of freezing it.

CHAPTER FIVE

Incest and Domestic Violence

With the advent of Pluto in Scorpio, incest, sexual molestation, child abuse, and domestic violence are all making headlines. The very week that Pluto went into Scorpio for the first time, in November, 1983, the television movie *Something About Amelia* was aired— the first really sensitive treatment of incest for a national audience. In the year that followed the news was full of developments about sexual abuse. Recent publicity about child pornography and about child molestation in day care centers has sickened all of us. A woman won a very large suit against her stepfather for molesting her, in what may become a landmark decision. Another young woman is suing several priests who molested her. A man won a huge settlement for psychological damages done when he was raped in jail. A self-help group was formed for women who have been sexually abused by their therapists.

In this chapter, we will discuss the psychological and astrological components of domestic violence, including incest, battered wives, and child abuse, all of which are extremely Plutonian in nature. As distressing as this material will be, it is a hundred times more distressing to the person who had to live it.

The Prevalence of Sexual Abuse
and Domestic Violence

More and more people are revealing that they were abused either physically or sexually. Abuse is probably the most underreported crime of all, because it is such a guilty secret for the victims. Even reported statistics and the very conservative estimates are overwhelming:

1. It is speculated that 20-40 percent of all girls between ages 4-13 will be sexually victimized by an adult.

2. 8 percent of boys have also been molested, but this is very much underreported because boys are afraid someone will think they aren't a man or are gay.

3. There are maybe 35 million people in this country who have been sexually molested.

4. Molestation is kept secret. Some 50-80 percent of the time, the person tells no one.

5. The offenders are male 80-90 percent of the time. 80 percent are close to the family in some way, rather than being a stranger.

6. 70 percent of young prostitutes are victims of incest or sexual abuse. 80 percent of female drug abusers have been sexually assaulted and use the drug to deaden their feelings.

7. In one study, 80 percent of the youngsters in a juvenile hall had been sexually assaulted.

8. At least 28 percent of all women are beaten by their husbands.

Sexual abuse and domestic violence cross all class and ethnic lines, yet are much more reported among the lower classes who have to depend on public agencies and city hospitals who keep statistics. A middle or upper class person can afford private medical and psychiatric care, and statistics are not made available.

Why this Chapter Is Necessary

As you can see, abuse is a major problem, not just something that happens to a few unfortunate people you never met. The reason for including it in a book on Pluto are twofold. First, abuse is a Plutonian problem and it creates Plutonian people. Second, this information is intended as in-service education for astrologers who may counsel victims.

Astrologers or counselors who see clients regularly should know the psychological effects of the victim experience and should be acquainted with local resources for incest survivors, battered wives, and rape victims. Your clients are going to be revealing their secrets as Pluto moves through Scorpio, so you need to be prepared to listen sensitively, understand their experience, and recommend places they can go for help. There will be those, also, who cannot reveal their secrets, who don't know yet that it is healing to talk about them. Recognizing the signatures in the chart may help you to gently and sensitively raise the issue, thus freeing the client to seek appropriate help.

The bibliography lists books about abuse that are all extremely upsetting to read. Yet, the pain of reading about abuse is nothing compared to the pain of the experience. The books would give you a thorough understanding of what abuse feels like, so that you can respond with empathy rather than making foolish judgements and assumptions. The authors articulate the experience better than most victims can.

Even if you are not an astrologer, you may find it useful to understand the victim, because the probabilities are very high that a neighbor, a friend, or even a family member will soon speak up about abuse that has been kept secret. Since one woman in three, and an unknown number of men, have suffered from some form of sexual abuse, you already know many of the victims personally, people who are suffering the effects in silence.

Our Tendency to Blame the Victim

One tendency we all have is to *blame the victim*. This often happens to victims of rape, as we judge that the woman must have worn provocative clothes or otherwise asked for it. It happens to the battered wife, when we play "junior Freudian" and decide that she must unconsciously provoke and desire her abuse out of some sick, masochistic need. It happens to incest victims, as we tend to think the child somehow seduced the parent or the quirky uncle. It happens to mugging victims, as we believe they were careless in being in that place at that time. We all want to believe—just as the victim does— that she or he somehow was responsible for what happened. Blaming the victim makes us feel more powerful, more in control, as though something like that could never happen to us. Sometimes the most vehement of blamers are those who have repressed memories of abuse done to them or who are repressing their own violent or antisocial urges.

There are lots of popular myths, all with the idea that victims love being abused, that they participate and contribute to it, and that's why they stay in the situation. No one understands, for instance, why the repeatedly battered wife doesn't just pick up and leave her husband, or why the victim of incest doesn't just tell her mother what is happening. If you read the histories or listen to the people, how- ever, you very often find that the battered wife did try to leave and the incest victim did try to tell someone, maybe more than once. The reactions of the family and key people in the environment, most especially the "helpers" in social agencies, the church, or the hospital were anything but helpful and ultimately pressed the women back into victimhood.

The consequence of this tradition of blaming the victim is that it adds to the isolation. Rape victims and battered wives, in particular, complain that the people they go to for help afterwards compound the damage with the insensitivity of their reactions. When people say it was your own fault, you become even more ashamed and enraged, so you shut up about it. It becomes a guilty secret that alienates you from the rest of humanity. In short, you become a Plutonian.

How the Oedipal Complex Got Invented

Another of the secrets revealed in the first year of Pluto's transit through Scorpio has to do with the origins of the Oedipal Complex. When Freud first began investigating neurosis, he wrote that it arose when children had sexual encounters with adults. This was not well received by his mentors and associates, so subsequently he "discovered" that this complex was entirely a fantasy on the part of females. Searching for the cause of these fantasies, Freud decided that it was because the female children wanted to sleep with their fathers (Eureka! The Oedipal Complex!) and when they could not, they had these fantasies in order to cope with the situation.

Lately, new information has come out about Freud and his circle of associates. It appears that Vienna was a Victorian hotbed of incest, child molesters, and child pornography. Freud's own trusted mentor, who urged him to abandon his early finding that molestation led to neurosis, was actually a child molester! Precisely like most men who molest children, if you read some of the books in the bibliography, he assured Freud that the children really wanted sex with adults, that they were seductive and "asking for it." Whether out of ambition (Scorpio Rising) or being too easily influenced by parental figures (Moon square Neptune), Freud bought it, and the Oedipal complex was born. Psychology was and is a male-dominated world, so male perspectives on sexuality are the ones which most influence our thinking.[20]

---

[20] If you are interested in reading more of the story, see Jeffrey M. Masson's *The Assault on Truth: Freud's Suppression of the Seduction Theory*, Farrar, Strauss & Giroux, NY, 1984.

Freud's chart was reproduced in Chapter Two (see Chart 3 on page 46). People's charts tell us what is going on with their work, even after they die. Freud's transits for 1983-6 are difficult, in that first Saturn in Scorpio and then Pluto opposes his strong, angular Pluto on the Descendant. The secret of the Pluto placement will out, even posthumously, and here the secret was the kind of associates he kept. The difficult transits he is going through in the 1980's suggest that Freud has fallen on hard times, and his popularity and influence will nosedive.

The problem with Freud's being duped is that he powerfully influenced all the generations of therapists since then, as well as those interested in pop psychology. Thus therapists and many interested lay people place the blame on the victim as the seductress, or dismiss the whole thing as fantasy. All too often, when children say someone is touching them where they shouldn't, a parent or other adult accuses the child of making it up. And yet no four or five year old child really has access to the details about sexuality that young victims describe.

Even when the children are believed, the theory of the guilty victim holds, so both therapists and pop psychologists often approach the victim from the viewpoint that the children unconsciously wanted the abuse and seduced the perpetrator. This tendency is alienating and enraging, increasing the guilt, resentment, and isolation the victims already feel. Another damaging tendency therapists have is blaming the mother, saying she was sexually frigid, driving the father to molest daughters because of her coldness. One reason Plutonians keep their secrets is that so often the people they go to for help wind up making them feel worse—more ashamed, more angry, and more betrayed.

Pluto, Masculine Power, and the Problem of Abuse

We will see a heightened and difficult Pluto in the charts of abuse victims. Sexual abuse and domestic violence are extremely Plutonian in nature, involving a traumatic betrayal of trust. It is essentially an abuse of power, particularly the almost total power of adult over child. With wife battering and rape, the perpetrator is still using superior power—fist power. With various forms of sexual abuse, it is not a question of simple lust, for that could always be satisfied in other ways. The real question is that of distorted power.

A distorted power complex is a major part of the psychology of men who commit physical or sexual abuse, according to interviews. These men are very much locked into a traditional male expectation of being dominant. Yet, something is happening in their lives so they can't live up to those cultural expectations—failing at work or otherwise—and they feel powerless. When they are totally frustrated over their lack of power in the world, they abuse their wives or children in order to feel powerful again. Very often, they, themselves, were abused as children, in an abuse of power that gets handed down through generations. Plutonians begat Plutonians.

Thus, the power relationships between the sexes set up the conditions for abuse in our culture and make it prominent. Children are raised to obey adults. Little girls, in particular, are raised to be docile, obedient, dependent, cooperative, and to defer to men. Thus girls are socialized in such a way that they are more likely to become victims, and the overwhelming number of victims are female. Women who are taught to be dependent on men, and who try to preserve a relationship at all costs, are also much more likely to stay with an abusive husband.

If you add up the statistics on battered wives, child abuse, rape, marital rape, and child molestation, it is a major social problem, one in which the overwhelming majority of perpetrators are male. It can no longer be seen as an individual problem, although the lives of individuals are tragically marred. It is a societal problem, and our society's expectations about men and women contribute to the problem in a major way. Pluto is as much about the masses and about social control as about the individual.

Another way in which abuse is Plutonian is that it often includes a revenge motif. Sometimes, for instance, rapists hate all women because of their mothers' sexual promiscuity or because of other things mothers did. When abusers were also abused children, they are seeking revenge for what was done. Often, if you look closely at incest, the father or brother is seeking revenge on the wife or parents and taking it out on the child. By acts of violence, perpetrators vent stored up rage, acting it out against someone who is powerless.

The Psychology of the Victim

Victims, by definition, have had overwhelming power used against them in a way they were helpless to resist. Victims of armed robbery, for instance, have no safe way to resist. Child abuse victims are helpless to prevent the repeated violence done to them. Incest victims and battered wives slowly, insidiously, have their power to resist taken from them as well.

Powerlessness does something to victims' personalities. Rage and fear get locked into their bodies, but if the abuse continues, they ultimately become numb. They come to feel that they were responsible, that they somehow provoked it, so they feel terribly guilty. (From Chapter Four, you will remember that guilt may arise out of the wish to feel you had power over a situation.) Paralysis sets in, especially when the abuse is repeated, so they feel helpless to do anything about it. Self-esteem is greatly lowered; these people feel tainted, as though no one would care for them if they knew. When they are not believed or helped, the abuse becomes a terrible, dirty secret. They come to feel they don't have rights—the right to say no, the right of control over their own bodies. Incest and sexual abuse victims in particular feel they haven't the right to say no sexually, since the violation of their bodies was done by an adult in authority over them.

Being the victim in one situation sets you up to be victimized in others as well. Having lost the sense of control over your life and your body, having lost the right to resist or to say no, you easily become the target for the next abusive person who comes along. Your posture is submissive; you are an easy mark for someone with a twisted power complex. Thus a woman who is battered by one husband may wind up marrying another man who beats her, prompting the pop psychologist to smirk self-righteously and say, "See, she unconsciously loves it!" Maybe she was a battered or molested child to begin with, setting up a pattern of being victimized.

Alcohol and Abuse

In certain studies, statistics show a strong correlation between alcohol abuse in a parent and other forms of abuse in the home. If the mother is an alcoholic, for instance, she is not so likely to be alert to sexual abuse happening to her children. Because of the irritability of the nervous system, which results from excessive use of alcohol, parents who drink are more prone to child abuse, and men who drink heavily are more likely to abuse their wives. About forty percent of cases in family court are due to alcoholism.

One reason for this is that there is an actual physical location in the brain called the inhibition center which governs impulse control. After heavy drinking, that center is numbed, and people may do things they wouldn't under normal circumstances. Regular excessive drinking can damage that center, so that, even when sober, these people are more prone to violence and to sexually inappropriate conduct. They cease to know right from wrong. Blackouts also occur in which alcoholics do things and genuinely don't remember them the next day. This is enraging, invalidating, and confusing to the victim. The liver, on the level of the energy body, is the organ that metabolizes anger, so alcoholics are resentful people. There can also be nerve damage, leaving them irritable.

For all these reasons, alcoholics are likely to abuse others in the family. Once again, there is the interplay between power and powerlessness, in that alcoholics feel powerless over alcohol and may turn to abuse as a way of feeling powerful and in control. Even where abuse does not happen in the home, however, children of alcoholics can be prime targets for victimization even as adults. Having been confronted with irrational authority figures whom they must placate in order to survive, and who often act bizarrely, these children are prone to submit to others who act similarly, even those who do not drink. As well, children of alcoholics marry alcoholics in at least thirty percent of the cases, and marrying an alcoholic can increase the potential for domestic violence.

I have done a great deal of work with adults who were children of alcoholics and find that they have Pluto strong in their charts, often stronger, in fact, than Neptune, the planet most associated with alcoholism. This shows how important the issue of control becomes when you have a parent who is frequently out of control. Even when abuse has not occurred, there are many emotional scars that come from such a background, traumas having to do with such Plutonian issues as lack of trust and fear of abandonment. An important self-help movement for adult children of alcoholics is rapidly spreading across the country.[21]

Sexual Abuse:
The Deepest, Darkest Secret

In something like forty-one percent of incest cases, the sexual abuse went on for an average of seven years. This prompts people to wonder why the children didn't just tell someone, why they didn't make it stop. Like most instances of repeated victimization, this is a complex question. Most survivors of repeated incest or molestation are gradually led into sexual acts by an adult whom they trust and are taught to obey. At first, the contact may be simply kissing and fondling, moving only slowly into overt genital touching, and per-haps years down the line into intercourse. Due to the manipulations and rationalizations the perpetrators use, it may be some time before the children truly understand that something wrong is going on. By the time they realize that this isn't something that happens to every-one, they feel guilty, afraid, and powerless to make it stop.

Usually the children are sworn to secrecy, with threats that something horrible will be done to them or someone they love. They may also be rewarded with gifts, money, and special favors. Often, these are children who aren't receiving much positive attention, so the affection and special attention is a kind of reward in itself. In addition, there is always the normal and natural love of the father or brother, which even severely battered children have, so it is confus-ing.

---

[21] Your local Alanon organization may have such groups, or you may find out more by writing to the National Organization of Children of Alcoholics, Box 421691, San Francisco, CA, 94142.

The children come to feel terribly guilty and powerful all at the same time. "Your mother won't do this for me. You're the only one who loves me. You're all I have." The children may feel that the family would be destroyed if they told—and very often this is exactly what would happen. If it is the father, he may be sent to jail or a mental institution, while the family also suffers financial destitution from the loss of his income. Sometimes the children are sent away to foster care, a further abandonment.

Thus, the terrible secret gives these children a strange sense of power in the midst of their powerlessness. It also creates a sense of total alienation, of being set apart from the family, the world outside, and most especially from the peer group. At the age of ten or eleven, when other girls are just beginning to giggle about boys, abused female children may be experiencing intercourse regularly. They feel alone in the world, not like other people, and can become depressed and withdrawn. Others act out their rage, becoming rebellious, delinquent, or sexually promiscuous. Others become young drug or alcohol abusers, or develop weight problems to avoid the issue of sexuality.

Case Examples of Incest

The charts which are reproduced here are gifts from two incest survivors I worked with in my private practice. (In the movement for women who have suffered from incestuous assault, it is preferred to call them survivors rather than victims.) If you can fathom how difficult it was to reveal this secret which haunted them most of their lives, you can appreciate what an act of courage it was for them to allow themselves to be written about in a book. Please send them a mental thank you.

Chart 6 on page 102 shows a client for whom I did a reading several years ago in New York. She says that I asked her whether some part of her problems in love relationships didn't have something to do with a difficult relationship with a brother, but that at that time she said, "Oh, no, everything was fine." Several years passed, and both of us moved to San Francisco, and she again came to me in late

1983. I looked at her difficult Saturn in Scorpio (in the third as part of a t-square with Venus and Mars), anticipating that she was going to be having her Saturn return. Not remembering what we discussed in the earlier reading, I again said that a very difficult relationship with a brother was behind the difficulties she experienced in relationships, and added that the Saturn return was the time to deal with it. At that point, she told me that her older brother had sexually abused her from age seven to fifteen. (Her brother was born 11/25/44, if you care to work with the synastry.)

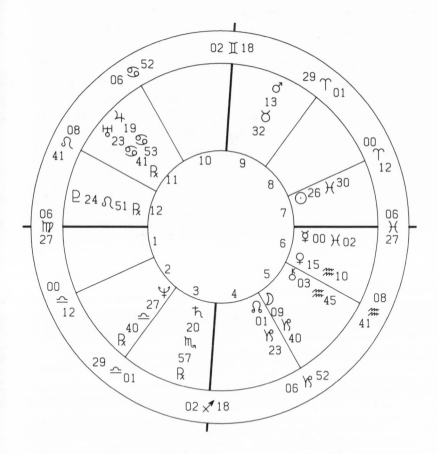

Chart 6. Female. Born New York, NY, March 17, 1955, 4:18 PM EST, tropical, Placidus. This is the chart of a woman who was sexually abused by her brother for many years. Data used with permission.

This is an important point for the astrologer to note. When I first did the chart, she was not ready to come forward with her secret, which stands out all over the chart once you know how to look for it. The Saturn in Scorpio in the third might in itself suggest abuse by a sibling, but when you tie it in with Venus, ruler of the third and Mars, ruler of the eighth, the indication is that the abuse was sexual. (Venus and Mars themselves, by nature, have to do with relationships and sexuality.) Additionally, Pluto is strong, in the twelfth house, within ten degrees of the Ascendant, being the intercepted ruler of the third, and it opposes Mercury, a natural indicator of a brother or sister. Another indicator might be the Neptune sitting on the cusp of the third, ruling the seventh, which, without the other aspects, might only show a tendency toward idealized love for a brother.

When a client is not ready to discuss the secret, it is extremely important not to push, although a general discussion of secrets and how toxic they are at another point in the reading may plant a seed for the future. When this woman again came to me for a reading, she was ready to open up because of severe distress in a relationship. Perhaps it also came about because I, too, was ready to hear it. In the meantime, I had done enough work with incest survivors and had enough experience in healing that I had something to offer. Then, too, the climate was right. *Something About Amelia* had aired on television; Pluto had moved into Scorpio and was trining her Mercury; and that strong Pluto of hers sensed the collective was more ready to help her.

And heal herself she did. Not only did we work together with the kinds of guided meditations and flower essences presented in this book, but she also read the books in the bibliography, had body work done, and joined a group for incest survivors. She went through a profound catharsis, months of deep turmoil of the sort typical to the process, and today she is doing work to help other incest survivors. She left an emotionally abusive relationship and is in a positive new one. (More information on the healing process will be given later.)

The second example (see Chart 7 on page 104) is also of a woman in my private practice who did a great deal of healing for herself by using meditations, flower essences, body work, and belonging to a group for incest survivors. She was sexually abused by her father from the age of seven to fourteen, when she went to her mother and confronted her with

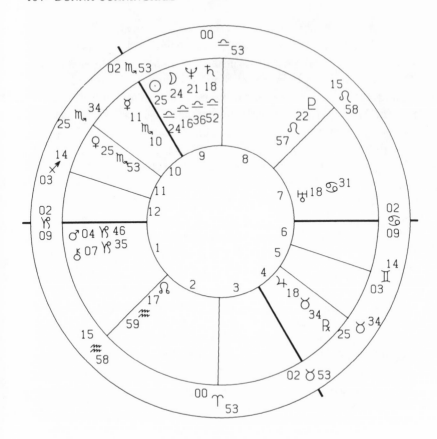

Chart 7. Female. Born Seattle, Washington, October 18, 1952, 12:23 PM PST, tropical, Placidus. This woman was sexually abused by her father from the age of seven until she was fourteen (see also Chart 8). Data used with permission.

what was going on. Her father was sent to a mental institution, and she herself was sent to a foster home.

The abuse shows up in the natal chart in several ways. Pluto, the ruler of the Midheaven, being placed in the eighth house does suggest a connection between a parent and the child's sexuality, although an astrologer would not conclude incest from this placement alone. It is conjunct the South Node in the eighth and in a t-square with Venus (the ruler of the fourth) and Jupiter in the fourth. These aspects tie sexuality and a parent closer together. You might infer some painful

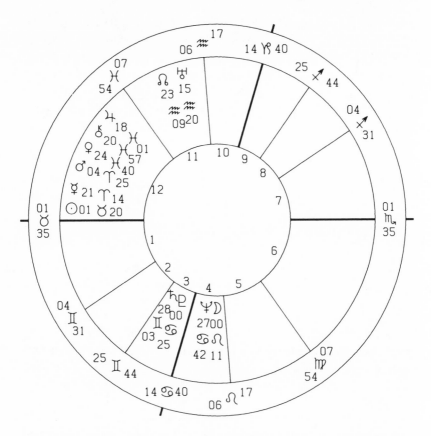

Chart 8. Solar chart of a father who sexually abused his daughter (see Chart 7). He was born April 22, 1915.

deception involving the parents with the Sun, Moon, Neptune, and Saturn all closely conjunct. Mars on the Ascendant is one signature of being sexually molested. (You may also note Chiron conjunct both.)[22] Her father's time of birth is unknown, but a solar chart for him is given as Chart 8. You may wish to work with the synastry.

---

[22] Chiron is included in all the charts in this book. We do not yet—at this writing—have a clear understanding of all the functions of this planetoid located between Saturn and Uranus, but the investigations of various astrologers suggest that the concept of the wounded healer may be valid.

The abuse began in 1959, when Neptune was going back and forth over her Scorpio Midheaven. She was able to stop the abuse in the Fall of 1966, when transiting Neptune was in the t-square and she was in too much pain to allow it go on longer. In terms of events in her life, her Midheaven appears slightly earlier than given here, probably about 1 Scorpio 30. She began actively working on this situation with me in January, 1984, as Pluto went over her Midheaven. (Individually and collectively, transiting Pluto has a tendency to go back and clear up what transiting Neptune brought all those years before.)

Healing Tools and Resources
for Incest Victims

Pluto in Scorpio not only shows secrets coming out in the open, it also shows the development of ways of healing these traumatic experiences. A major self-help movement for incest survivors began during the Pluto/Saturn conjunction of 1982-83, and is gaining momentum as Pluto moves through Scorpio. Incest is perhaps the most toxic of the deep, dark secrets, the one with the most shame and stigma, and thus the one that most needs groups where survivors can talk openly about their secret. Because of the group support, this form of healing is one of the more effective contributions.

In these self-help and therapy groups, survivors have the opportunity to tell their secret and discuss various aspects of their feelings with others who have lived through it. This group experience is powerfully healing. Many of the groups recommend and support the survivor in bringing the secret out into the open with the family, including, in many cases, a confrontation with the perpetrator. A side effect is that this frees other family members to tell their secrets as well—very often there is more than one generation of abuse involved.

An interestingly Scorpionic tendency in the movement is to demand that the perpetrator make restitution in some way. There is no amount of money that could compensate for the damage, but often the demand is made—and accepted—that the perpetrator pay for the therapy, and survivors find this exchange healing. Often, it is insisted that the perpetrator himself get therapy. The women in Charts 6 and 7 had family conferences and insisted that their therapy be paid for, yet neither felt they would have been able to do so without group support. (Where money for therapy is not available in this way, crime victim assistance programs in certain cities have paid for it, even when the incest was never reported.)

Body work is another essential part of the healing for survivors. The repeated violation may have made them shut off from their bodies, and also may have caused them to have emotional residuals (fear, rage, sadness) in the muscles and body tissues. Body work releases stored emotions and allows them to reclaim their enjoyment of their bodies. Naturally, it might be hard to allow male therapists to work on them, and it might also be unwise to go through some of the more painful forms of body work, like rolfing, where the pain could translate emotionally as simply another period of abuse.

Books can be healing, too, especially for people who think they are alone in their terrible secret. Sometimes these women need to read books like the ones in the bibliography in order to understand they are not unusual. This realization begins to cut through the isolation, so they can be more open to working with a group and to telling others about it. The books serve another purpose, in that they induce a catharsis of frozen feelings about the experiences.

A period of catharsis seems to happen to most incest survivors as they become ready to work on the problem, an intense version of the healing crisis discussed in Chapter Three. Crying, rage, and fear come up, feelings people may have cut off for years. (Begins to sound just like a Pluto transit, doesn't it?) Things may be pretty rocky for a while. There is no escape, but there is relief in dealing with it at last, and when this awful secret is shared, it brings a sense of hope that the future can be better for working it through. There is a period of telling the secret to anyone they feel cares enough to listen. Survivors also find other appropriate situations to tell it in, like incest speakouts. Telling it and telling it and telling it is part of the healing, because the sense of being set apart lessens with each telling.

While talking about it helps, healing has to proceed on many different levels. Thus the flower remedies and guided meditations in this book can play an important part in clearing out the damage. Bach remedies seem to be more important here. Star of Bethlehem for old traumas, Honeysuckle for letting go of the past, Holly for hate, and Willow for resentment are all very important. Centaury, for passivity and not being taken advantage of, helps with the victim stance. Within the California essences, the ones for sexuality may be needed when the healing is further along. Sticky Monkeyflower for fear of intimacy and for integrating sexual energies could be very useful; others might include Fig for trust between couples, Manzanita for ambivalence about the body and for grounding, and Fuschia for integrating powerful emotions.

A Case of Child Abuse

The following case of child abuse came to my attention a number of years ago, when I wrote advice columns for astrology magazines. At that time, I was Director of Social Service in a hospital, and while arranging a series of educational programs about child abuse for the staff, I was struck by how Plutonian the relationships were—the power struggles, the revenge motif, the deep dark secret. All these dynamics will be seen in the sad case considered here. The story itself reeks of Pluto, even before you look at the charts involved.

The story and birth information were given to me by the grandmother, but names and birth information will be concealed for reasons of confidentiality. All information is presented from the grandmother's point of view. I did not meet the people, since they lived in another state. Nonetheless, when talking to the grandmother on the phone, she seemed to be a stable person and a reliable source of information.

The family consisted of four people: an abusive father and mother, the abused older child, and the adored younger child who was not abused. We will look at individual charts and composites. This case represents an unusual opportunity to see all the charts rather than just that of the abused individual. Child abuse is a family problem, in which all members play a part, and in which the abused child has been given a particular role. We will call the boy Jeremy III. It is significant that his grandfather was Jeremy Sr. and his father Jeremy II. The names alone might indicate that some displaced rage at both the grandfather and father is being acted out in the beatings.

This child was the product of a forced marriage when the mother, whom we will call Alice, became pregnant. It can be suspected, even from the charts, that she deliberately got pregnant to trap the father into marriage. (Pluto is in the father's fifth, which often suggests a pregnancy marriage, and there is a heavy Pluto and Scorpio influence in the mother's chart, which we will see later.) From her chart, we might also suspect she did this out of desperation, to escape from her own abusive parents. Immediately after the marriage, she sought an illegal abortion. She was not successful and hated the child from the time he was born. The father bitterly resented marriage and parenthood, as he wasn't ready for the responsibility and wanted to go to medical school. He ultimately did go, and was a surgical resident at the time the grandmother wrote to me. (What about the Hippocratic Oath, fella, my Pluto wants to ask!)

Both parents beat the child from toddlerhood onward. Serious physical and emotional damage was done, including a broken arm, testicles so badly injured that surgery was required, and a period where he could not even walk and had to learn all over again. (Hopefully, by now, no hospital would observe injuries like that and not become suspicious.) Emotional damage was apparent, in that the child shook continually, was often withdrawn from reality, and was jumping from high places. The relationship between the parents was a strange, sado-masochistic one. The mother was promiscuous, and the child often witnessed her having sex with other men. The father once caught her in bed with another man who held him and the children at gunpoint. After that incident, the parents divorced but still lived together.

The couple had a second child, three years younger, whom we shall call Charles. In stark contrast, Charles was adored, showered with attention and possessions. They seemed to have split their ambivalent feelings about parenthood right down the middle. It is not unusual in such families to have only one of the children abused—the abused child is special, sometimes demanding more care or coming at a crisis time when the parents can't meet the demands of an infant, or possibly resembling someone a parent hates.

The grandparents were extremely worried about Jeremy III. At one point, when the child was visiting, they took him to a pediatrician who reported the case to child welfare authorities. Their efforts were blocked because the parents were able to put up a good front to investigators, being outwardly charming and quite intelligent, as well. The father's position as a doctor-to-be also shielded him; physicians are reluctant to see any mental problem in a fellow physician and are notorious for covering up for one another. The only result was that the grandparents were not allowed to visit for a year, and the boy was even more seriously abused in retaliation. Understandably, the grandparents were reluctant to take further action, feeling it might endanger the child and their relationship even more. However, at the time the grandmother wrote to me, both the natal charts and coming transits were alarming, so I advised her to seek legal help to remove the child. The outcome is unknown.

The beginning astrology student may find the interpretations which follow quite technical. Unfortunately there is little that could be done without depriving practicing astrologers of important information they might need some day. You would be advised to get as much as you can from the psychological exposition or skip to the more general chapters.

JEREMY III: THE ABUSED CHILD

Chart 9 is extremely Plutonian, in that Pluto and Uranus are conjunct in the eighth house, forming a t-square with an opposition to a Mars/Saturn

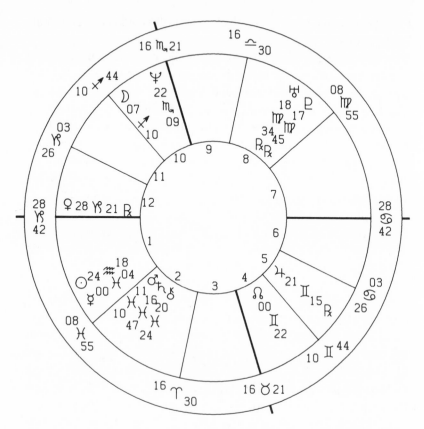

Chart 9. Jeremy III, an abused child. The birth data is not available for reasons of confidentiality.

conjunction squared by Jupiter. Mars/Uranus, Mars/Saturn, and Mars/Pluto aspects can all show a brutal parent, and to have all three is singularly difficult. The eighth house location of this very difficult Pluto, ruler of the Midheaven, would raise the possibility of sexual abuse as well, since some cases of incest have similar signatures. The Midheaven, which shows the parents as authority figures, is in Scorpio, and Neptune in Scorpio is conjunct it and square his Sun. Neptune there suggests emotional disturbance on the part of the parents, but also their ability to put up a false front. Alcohol or drugs could play a part in the family violence.

The severely difficult aspects in the chart far outweigh the helpful ones, but Jupiter in the fifth, trine the Sun, suggests that help may come through the school and from legal assistance. Venus in Capricorn on the Ascendant ruling the ninth and the fourth also suggests that legal intervention by the grandparents could save him. Nonetheless, the damage suggested by that t-square and prominent Neptune square the Sun is considerable. As often happens, he himself could be abusive or violent as an adult, unless he received a great deal of therapy. Pluto is strong in the chart, so healing could occur, but only with a great deal of work.

ALICE: THE ABUSIVE MOTHER

Of the parents' charts, Alice's appears by far the more abusive. (See Chart 10.) She was born with the rather infamous Pluto-Saturn conjunction in Leo closely conjunct her Leo Midheaven, showing her as a person who must dominate at all costs. This combination also suggests that she herself may have had a power-hungry and abusive parent, and that her abuse of Jeremy may be a way of acting out her hatred and vengeance toward that parent. The square from Jupiter in Scorpio in the first only expands the desire for power. She has Scorpio rising and Venus and Mercury in Scorpio as well. Her highly sexual nature may arise from this concentration of Plutonian energy, but its first/tenth house concentration suggests she may have been excessively stimulated at an early age by events concerning her parents. Of the two parents, her chart more clearly illustrates the finding that an abused child can grow up to become an abusive parent. (The grandmother, who was her mother-in-law, had no information on Alice's childhood.)

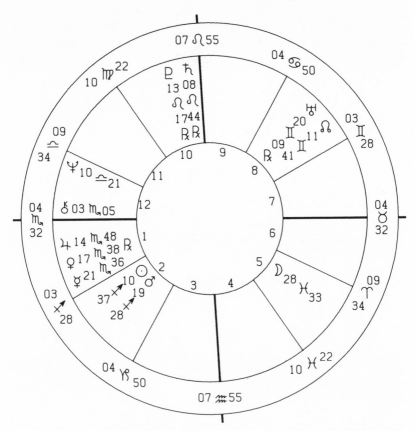

Chart 10. Alice, the abusive mother who gave birth to Jeremy III. Readers should refer to Chart 9 for the planetary ties between mother and son. Birth data is not available for reasons of confidentiality.

Exactly like her son, Alice has a difficult t-square involving a Mars/Uranus opposition from the eighth house, forming squares to a planet in the fifth, the house of children. In her case, the fifth house planet is her Pisces Moon, suggesting that she feels trapped and enraged by the need to nurture others. The same degrees of the mutable signs are involved as in Jeremy's chart, so the synastry shows he could readily be a target for her explosive anger. The eighth house

Uranus aspected by Mars suggests that for her, somehow, violence has become sexualized, so there can be a heavily sexual undercurrent to the beatings, an S&M component.

COMPOSITE CHART: ALICE AND JEREMY III

The mathematical principles of composite charts are such that whenever both people have *any* aspect between two given planets, the

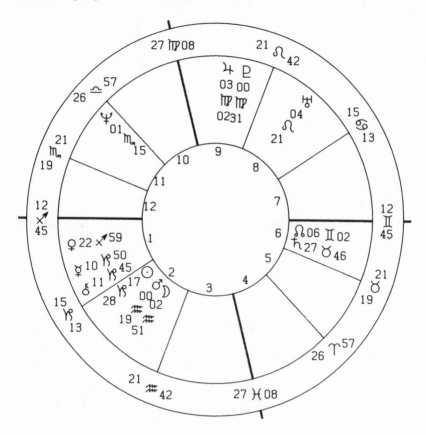

Chart 11. The composite chart combining Alice (Chart 10) and her son, Jeremy III (Chart 9).

composite will have some kind of aspect between those same two planets. A Mars/Uranus opposition from the eighth to the second appears in both Jeremy's and Alice's charts, so the composite (Chart 11) has the same aspect, again in a t-square, this time to Neptune, with the Moon conjunct Mars. The t-square is in fixed signs, which are more entrenched in their behavior, and more resistant to change. The Moon is in Aquarius, a rather explosive Moon at times, particularly with Mars and Uranus forming such difficult aspects.

Pluto is also significant, in that a close Jupiter/Pluto conjunction forms quincunxes to the Moon and Mars in Aquarius, sesquiquadrates to the Sun, and a square to Saturn. The Pluto/Saturn square echoes the mother's own Pluto/Saturn conjunction and Jeremy's Pluto/Saturn opposition. Since Pluto and Jupiter are in the ninth house, legal remedy is again suggested.

JEREMY II: THE ABUSIVE FATHER

Jeremy III's father is shown in Chart 12 on page 116. He also has difficult placements in the mutable signs, in some of the same degrees, but not a t-square. Mars and Uranus are conjunct. The fact that Mars and Uranus are in Gemini and on the cusp of the third house (brothers and sisters), squaring the Moon, hints that what may be going on in his angry explosions is a kind of sibling rivalry with his son. This is echoed by the strong fifth house placements, including the Sun. Many strongly fifth house people want to be indulged children themselves, not saddled with children.

Mars and Uranus square his Pisces Moon in the twelfth, which is also opposite Jupiter and near Alice's Pisces Moon. Thus there is some suggestion that he is strongly negatively influenced by her, and that his behavior toward his son is a way of acting out his rage at his wife. Unconsciously, she is seen as a mother figure, and his rage is at frustrated dependency needs. Again, given the strong Neptunian component, there is the possibility that drugs or alcohol may trigger the abuse.

Pluto is less dominant in this chart, but falls into the house of children, the fifth house. It is virtually unaspected, which can in itself bespeak difficulty in integrating that energy into the life. (Paradoxically, an unaspected planet can become dominant.) There is a wide sesquiquadrate to the Pisces Moon, again suggesting that he is acting out revenge on his wife, even possibly on his mother.

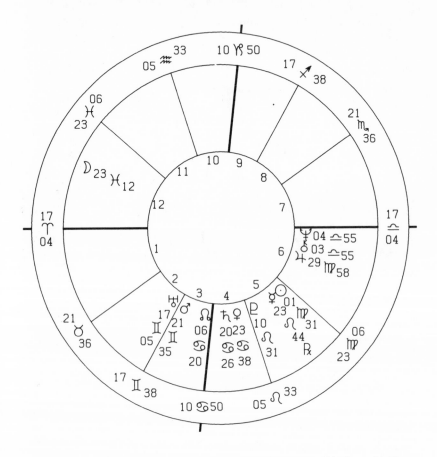

Chart 12. Jeremy II, the abusive father. Readers should compare this chart with Chart 9 to see the ties between father and son. Birth data is not available for reasons of confidentiality.

COMPOSITE CHART: JEREMY III AND HIS FATHER

Chart 13 is a composite and is even more difficult than the composite between Jeremy and his mother. Rather than a t-square, there is a grand cross spread across the fixed and cardinal signs. Once more, the Moon, Mars, Uranus, and Neptune are part of it, joined here by Venus. The eighth house and Pluto are again featured. Pluto closely squares the Scorpio Sun and forms a quincunx to the Moon. Pluto is angular, close to the Descendant.

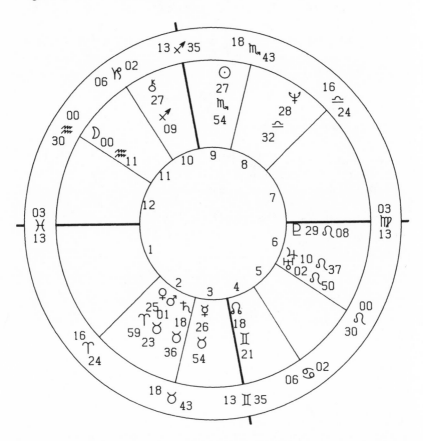

Chart 13. The composite chart combining Jeremy II (the father in Chart 12) with his son, Jeremy II (Chart 9).

COMPOSITE CHART: PARENTS

Since both parents have Pisces Moons with hard aspects to Mars and Uranus, their composite (see Chart 14) does too, forming still another mutable t-square, along with Venus and the Nodes. The eighth house is important, containing one end of the t-square, with Pluto near the cusp of the eighth, sesquiquadrate the Moon. There is no doubt that for this couple the violence is sexualized, and that they have a sado-masochistic relationship. With four planets in the ninth house, legal complications seem likely, yet the Sun/Jupiter conjunction shows they could grow from it.

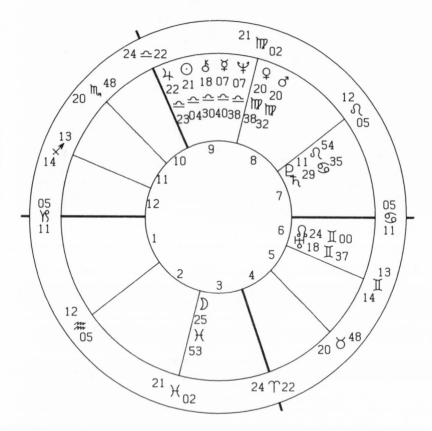

Chart 14. The composite chart for the parents, Alice and Jeremy II. (See Charts 10 and 12.)

CHARLES: THE FAVORED SON

Chart 15 is by no means an easy chart. It is full of quincunxes, including an Eye of God formation with the Sun at the apex. Quincunxes bespeak incongruities or difficulties reconciling one need with another. With the Sun and Saturn in Aries conjunct the Midheaven, and Leo Rising, Charles needs and wants attention, but it is an uneasy crown he wears. The quincunxes to Neptune and Pluto show the undercurrents and the deception that is going on, all of which should give him the uneasy sense that the love he is getting may not be real, that he had better be perfect or he might be next.

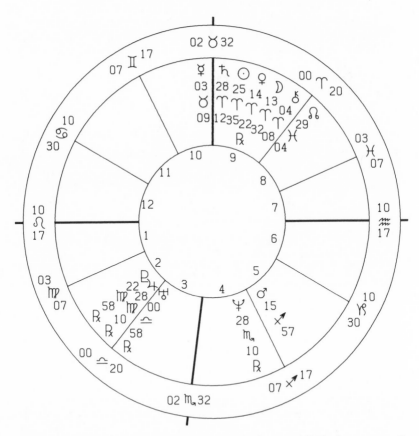

Chart 15. Charles, the favored child, Birth date is not available for reasons of confidentiality.

With Leo rising, the Eye of God with the Sun, and all his elevated planets, Charles has been given an elevated view of himself as a very special person (he may literally feel that the eye of God is upon him), yet, with no squares or oppositions to galvanize him into action, he doesn't know what to do to attain or deserve that lofty position his parents are setting him up to expect. The eye of God is repeated in Charles's composite with his father, which is shown as Chart 16.

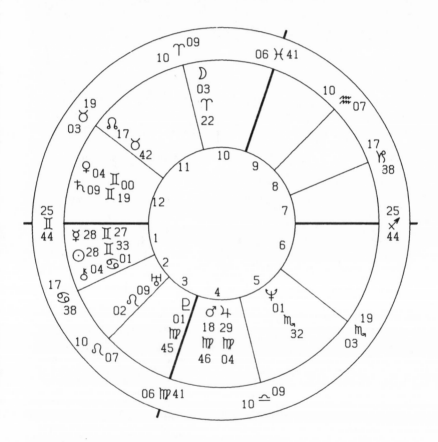

Chart 16. The composite chart for Charles and his father, Jeremy II. (See Charts 12 and 15.)

We have seen the charts of all four family members in a case of severe child abuse, as well as composite charts illustrating the complex relationships between various members. Certain common themes and even common degrees were remarked upon. Most especially, those involved in the abuse had difficult aspects in the mutable signs, all with Mars/Uranus and Mars/Moon hard aspects. T-squares with these planets appeared in both natal and composite charts. The eighth house was prominent, as was Pluto, illustrating the sexualization of violence and the warping of power and control needs. We should not conclude that any of these placements, on their own, lead to child abuse, but the extreme concentration of difficult aspects, all interlocked in the charts of family members, did result in severe abuse.

Some Healing Ideas

If you have been abused, perhaps it would be healing to start a group yourself. Some of the healing tools in this book could be helpful, such as the exercises for guilt and resentment. Doing exactly the same exercise as the one for resentment, but using the color blue, would help to remove the residue of fear. GENTLE body work, such as massage, not the painful ones like rolfing, could help release the stored up emotions and give you a pleasurable sense of your body. Bach flower remedies which could help are Star of Bethlehem (for old shocks and traumas), Honeysuckle (for letting go of the past), Willow (for resentment and bitterness), Holly (for hatred, suspicion, and the desire for revenge), and Centaury (not to allow further victimization). An important self-help group for adults who suffered from physical abuse as children has been formed by Christina Crawford, who wrote *Mommy Dearest*. You may contact them by writing to The Survivors Network, 18653 Ventura Boulevard #143, Tarzana, CA 91356.

Some Final Words on Abuse

No doubt you have found this chapter quite depressing, yet if you practice astrology, you may run into cases this severe, and you will need to understand both the astrology and the psychology of child abuse and molestation. If it is depressing for you, you can imagine how nightmarish it would be for the people involved, so your understanding and compassion, your ability to hear what the person has to say without being freaked out, is quite important. With Pluto in Scorpio, more and more victims of various forms of abuse will be opening up their secrets to you and to other kinds of healers and helpers. The books in the bibliography which follows can prepare you to understand and be helpful, as well as to know what treatment is available to heal the aftermath.

Books About Incest and Molestation

Armstrong, Louise. *Kiss Daddy Goodnight*. Hawthorne, N.Y., 1978. Case histories of a number of incest survivors, gathered by a survivor. Powerful and painful.

Brady, Katharine. *Father's Days: A True Story of Incest*. Seaview Books, N.Y., 1979. One woman's story of incest, including what happened as an adult when she decided to confront the situation.

Butler, Sandra. *Conspiracy of Silence: The Trauma of Incest*. Volcano Press, San Francisco, 1978. An excellent book on the subject, including interviews with survivors, their mothers, and the perpetrators. Failings of the helping professions in dealing with this problem.

Morris, Michelle. *If I Should Die Before I Wake*. Dell, N.Y., 1982. An extremely well-written novel about a teenage incest victim, stunningly accurate in detail.

Rush, Florence. *The Best Kept Secret: Sexual Abuse of Children.* McGraw Hill, N.Y., 1980. A painful, well-written book about various psychological, sociological, and historical facets of child sexual abuse.

Books About Rape

Brownmiller, Susan. *Against Our Will: Men, Women, and Rape.* Simon and Schuster, N.Y., 1975. Classic feminist text on rape as an expression of men's hostility toward women and the imbalance of power between the sexes.

Books About Domestic Violence

Martin, Dell. *Battered Wives.* Pocket Books, N.Y. Revised, 1983. The earliest book on wife abuse, which sparked a great growth of consciousness and a movement to help these victims.

McNulty, Faith. *The Burning Bed.* Harcourt Brace Jovanovich, N.Y., 1983. The story of Francine Hughes, who killed her abusive husband and was acquitted in a landmark decision. (Made into a television movie during 1984, less than a year after Pluto entered Scorpio.) Francine was a 1947 Leo, born during the Pluto/Saturn conjunction in Leo, but the book does not pinpoint her exact date of birth.

Walker, Lenore E. *The Battered Woman.* Harper and Row, N.Y., 1979. Case histories and the psychology of the victim, as well as information on treatment.

CHAPTER SIX

Death and the Transformative Power of Grief

The ideas we will examine in this chapter apply not only to grief because of a death, but also to the loss of a relationship, a career setback, an ability that is no longer there, and most especially to the ending of a dream or hope that was part of the reason for being. Death is the purer case, easier to grasp, but it is equally important to mourn other losses too. By looking at this difficult topic, we will learn how very Plutonian mourning is. It often involves guilt, resentment, holding on, wanting to control, and the desire for revenge. Pluto rules both death and transformation, and the death of someone meaningful is often a time of transformation, but only as we allow ourselves to mourn. Healing tools for dealing with grief will be presented at the end of the chapter.

Although it goes against the natural reticence of my Pluto/ Ascendant conjunction to make it public, I am a medium. Not only is some of my material channelled, but I also have the capacity to communicate with people who have died, as an inevitable consequence of being around death. I don't practice mediumship for members of the general public who are curious and want to know how grandma likes the afterlife, but I have willingly acted as a medium when it was indicated in the course of therapy with people—Plutonians mainly—who were in considerable pain due to a death they were unable to resolve. In such instances, mediumship is a form of healing, the therapy of choice. A case example will be included later on.

Given this determinedly nonprofessional standpoint, my experience with mediumship is limited yet rather consistent. Keep in mind that it is only one person's experience, mixed with study and talking with professional mediums. Not exactly by coincidence, while this chapter was in process, the Universe collaborated by arranging a stay with a famous European medium in London, who took me around to functions of the Spiritualist church and taught me a great deal about classical mediumship. The Universe also provided exposure to a couple of deaths while this was being written, but it was hard to be grateful for that particular bit of help.

How Grief Became Gauche

With the Moon in Aquarius in the US chart, we don't know how to grieve. More and more, we are expected to be detached, to pretend the loss doesn't matter. "He's taking it very well," is considered a compliment, rather than a matter for concern. If you are so gauche as to mourn for more than a couple of months for your loss, transformation junkies will ask you, in essence if not in fact, "Where does it get you to hold on to that?" Now that we're all a bit spiritually aware, we add superficial information on life after death to our list of reasons for mourning being passe. "You're only holding her back by carrying on so, my dear. Don't you see you must let her go so she can make her transition?" These statements are not wisdom, but sophistry, and are a way to cop out on what psychotherapists call grief work.

Another glib copout is to minimize the loss (especially someone else's) by glorifying death as an instant release and wonderful enlightenment. "How wonderful that he has found his release." The deceased are often every bit as unenlightened as they were in life, even years afterward. Their healing is NOT instant—it can take up to two years to get the astral body in shape. Possibly at the moment of death, it is as described in the research, with lights and awesome spiritual presences and so on, but after the honeymoon period, the adjustment to having passed over takes time, especially for those who have as little preparation as people in our culture.

Once there were customs for mourning which helped the survivor work through grief, and which doubtlessly helped the deceased in understanding and accepting what had happened. Many of these customs, even within the framework of traditional religions, were intuitively based on sound occult principles and knowledge about what happens after death. Black, for instance, acts as a psychic shield and protects the mourner from being overwhelmed by mediumistic contact with the departed. It seems to take about a year after death to pass over to a second level of greater detachment from our plane; the traditional mourning period lasted for a year, masses were said, and the bereaved were protected and removed from social responsibilities. A year or two is the most intense part of a Pluto transit, and often a Pluto transit accompanies the death of someone or something meaningful. (Not every Pluto transit means a death, but every one does mean an end to something major.)

Death and the Pluto in Leo Generation

Pluto often carries the theme of abandonment, and we modern folk (the Pluto in Leo crew) selfishly abandon the dying, leaving them isolated, rather than dealing with our feelings about death. We also self-centeredly abandon the dead and those who mourn them. In the beginning, at least, the dead can miss us as profoundly as we miss them and can feel isolated when we do not give them our loving grief. So what if your dear old mother and your favorite Uncle Bill are there on the other side to greet you when you die? It doesn't entirely make up for intimate contact with the loved ones you left behind who now aren't talking to you because they don't know how or—worse— don't even know you continue to exist. Dying is sort of like moving away, except you don't get as many letters from your friends.

The Pluto in Cancer generation were better at nurturing those in mourning, but the Pluto in Leo generation only notices what a bummer it is to be around them. "It's just too draining. I have to take care of myself." The generation with Pluto in Virgo and Neptune in Scorpio, as they become the caretaking adults in our culture, will doubtlessly be devoted and capable helpers of the dying and their survivors. Since Neptune has to do with psychic abilities, and Scorpio (like Pluto) with mediumship, this should be a generation of natural mediums, the time in history when communication with the afterlife becomes a natural and accepted thing.

In defense of the Pluto in Leo people, it is well to consider why they are so callous about death. Doubtlessly, it is because they have seen so much of it. They were born during a devastating World War or in its aftermath, followed closely by Korea. On top of all that, the perpetual threat of nuclear annihilation began shortly after they were born. When they were young adults or teenagers, they were confronted with Vietnam and the senseless masses of deaths in a war they couldn't believe in. Television shows average several brutal killings an hour, giving the message that life is cheap. A time comes when we can no longer take it in, when we have suffered loss, or the threat of it, so many times that we close down to it. As La Rochefoucauld said, "Death and the sun are not to be looked at steadily." This continual exposure to the possibility of annihilation may also be part of the reason for the Pluto in Leo generation's hedonism; "Eat, drink, and be merry, for tomorrow you may die."

That generation will be getting transiting Pluto in Scorpio square natal Pluto at about the age of forty-two. It is a generation of unusual resentment toward parents, and as their parents begin dying, it should be an important transformational crisis. The narcissism that this so-called "me generation" is known for should be changing, through exposure to mortality, to a greater concern for the whole.

Elisabeth Kübler-Ross
and the Liberation of the Dying

The 1960s were marked by the conjunction of Uranus and Pluto in the sign Virgo, a combination that brought a great many social reform and liberation movements. One of the most beautiful was that led by Elisabeth Kübler-Ross to ensure the rights of the dying to compassionate and understanding treatment. Like most Plutonian areas of life, death is often taboo to talk about, and her work opened the way for communication with those who are in the process of dying. Like many Plutonians, Elisabeth suffered oppressive and underhanded attacks as the establishment attempted to maintain the status quo. The medical world was forever trying to dig up scandal, trying to say that she was insane. Doctors, being healers, are Plutonians, and as such have difficulty with death's reminder of their ultimate powerlessness.

Even at this point, Kübler-Ross goes through periodic conflicts with the powers that be. The psychic and mediumistic opening that she has been through in recent years has again resulted in rumors of insanity. Through her experiences with dying patients and with patients who communicated after death, she has come to believe deeply in survival past death and in reincarnation. In the epilogue to her biography, she says:

> I have had every mystical experience that human beings are capable of. I have experienced the greatest highs without ever having taken drugs. I have seen the light that my patients see in their near-death experiences, and I have been surrounded by that incredible unconditional love that all of us experience when we make the transition called death.[23]

As you can see from Chart 17 on page 130, Elisabeth Kübler-Ross qualifies as a Plutonian. She has Pluto conjunct her Cancer Sun and

---

[23] Derek Gill, *Quest: The Life of Elisabeth Kübler-Ross*, Harper & Row, NY, 1980, p. 378.

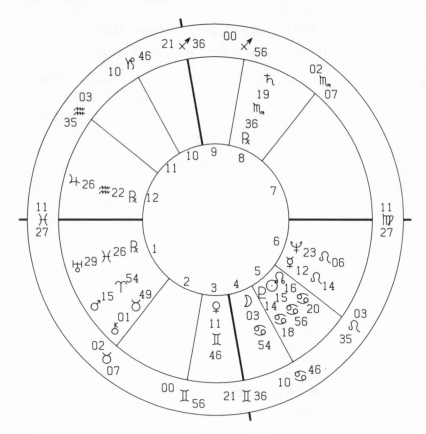

Chart 17. Elisabeth Kübler-Ross. Born Zurich, Switzerland, July 8, 1926, 22:45, tropical, Placidus. Data supplied by Lois Rodden, and this birth time is more recent than that used in her book, *Profiles of Women* (AFA, Tempe, AZ, 1979).

North Node and very widely conjunct her Cancer Moon. What higher expression of this combination could there be than in her nurturing and caring for the dying? If you gave me the chart and didn't identify her, I would guess her profession as a medium, so strong are the mediumistic indications. The close square from Mars in Aries in the first house to Pluto and the Sun is difficult, yet she uses it in the highest expression, as a fighter and leader for the rights of the dying. (Quite possibly, however, she does provoke some of the battles she gets into with the powers that be.) The Sun and Pluto are trine Saturn in Scorpio in the eighth house, showing that she would take this as a professional responsibility and become a healer in this area.

What to Expect from Grief

It may be useful to describe what grief is like, so you will know if someone is in a grief state. It's a very Plutonian state of mind, for grieving people struggle not to show their feelings outwardly, because others tend to shun them if they go into it too intensely. There is often a good deal of isolation: for instance, widows often find that the former friends of the couple no longer want a single woman around. There is often obsessive thinking about the deceased, and, as we will consider later, a great deal of guilt and resentment. Sometimes the wish to die is strong. The person may feel abandoned and betrayed by the person who died, friends, and God.

There may be an initial period of numbness and shock; grieving people can go through the funeral ritual and the weeks immediately after in a zombie-like state. ("She's taking it so well.") Doctors and friends with well-stocked medicine cabinets or private stashes contribute to this numbness by insisting on sedating grieving people. One suspects it is done not so much out of concern for the bereaved (who need to experience their feelings to complete the process of mourning), but in order not to have to be around such unpleasant feelings themselves. This practice is most unwise, as the grief easily gets pushed down into the unconscious. Also, being able to feel grief at the time when the loss occurs means that grieving people get more social validation than weeks, months, or even years later, when the feelings do eventually surface. (Some people may be hard put to get any social validation at all if the relationship is a Plutonian one, secret or not socially sanctioned—like a gay lover, a long-term relationship with a married man, or your alcoholic father whom everyone else disowned years ago.)

Grief is a powerful emotion, possibly the most intense. The intensity would vary depending on the strength of the bond (either positive or negative), how Plutonian the relationship was, how prepared you were for the death, or how acceptable or how Plutonian the death (suicide, cancer, and murder being more Plutonian). In acute grief, you may wake up in the middle of the night, night after night, in a state of anguish, and who can you call at a time like that? (Insomnia seems to accompany many Pluto transits, perhaps because there is mourning about a death or a rebirth.)

In addition to sleeplessness and deep sorrow, there may be physical symptoms like loss of appetite, dizziness, a pain or leaden feeling in the chest. The chest sensation, which may frighten people into thinking they are dying too, comes from the wound to the heart center that accompanies a major loss. The heart center (or chakra) is a part of the aura that governs the giving and taking in of love energy. When the heart center is wounded, it closes down for a time, so that even if others are trying to give love, grieving people often cannot take it in, increasing the isolation. Use the exercise in Chapter Three to reopen the heart chakra. (If the death was caused by a heart or lung condition, the survivor may also be picking up the symptoms mediumistically.)

Grief feelings seem to come and go. At times we forget and immerse ourselves in living. Then, the smallest thing—an object that belonged to the deceased, a song they loved, a view they enjoyed— brings it all back in a breathtaking blow. Dealing with personal effects is the hardest thing, yet doing it and precipitating the mourning over each little shared reality is actually healing. Holidays and other special occasions may bring grief rushing back. Especially well known to psychotherapists is the anniversary reaction, for depressions may occur year after year at the time of the loved one's death, and often we are unaware we are mourning. (Pluto may be back in the same approximate position a year later.)

Worst of all is the isolation, for no one really understands, and no one really wants to make more than a token visit to assuage their own guilt. Grieving people need to be touched and held, and if the loved one was a mate, that comfort may be denied unless other sensitive people provide for it. There may also be times when we are sexually needy, for death increses our desire to hold on to the physical, yet we feel guilty and disloyal for wanting this release. (All the meanings of Pluto seem to arise in bereavement, don't they?)

When a past death or other loss has not been thoroughly mourned, a new loss may activate held-in grief. A Pluto transit may coincide with a loss, but not always. Some people under Pluto transits may freshly experience and deeply mourn an old loss, which current life circumstances force them to confront. Even though these periods can be excruciatingly painful, they bring the possibility of resolving a loss or death so life can begin again where it left off. In the process, people may need to experience the abandonment, resentment, guilt, a sense of betrayal, or all the feelings they couldn't work through when the loss or death actually occurred.

Harvard University has done an extensive study of grief, as reported in the book *Recovery From Bereavement*. Some further Plutonian insights were gained from this study, for extreme dependency of the symbiotic type made the loss much more difficult to deal with. The report also indicated that some people were unable to function independently, and they had a sense of hopelessness about the future. In addition, survivors of bad marriages had an extremely difficult time getting over the death—often overwhelming grief went on for years. Not only did death mean the loss of hope of things ever getting better in the relationship, but an overwhelming amount of guilt and resentment can be mixed with grief in such situations.[24]

Resentment as a Component of Grief

Psychotherapists find that grief carries with it resentment toward the deceased for the abandonment. At some level, we perceive that the soul of the individual has chosen its time and manner of death, and we are furious that they chose to leave us, even though most of the time the choice has nothing to do with us. We are not allowed to feel this rage—it's not nice! The resentment about the abandonment does get acted out, not toward the one who died, but toward our fellow survivors. We displace our anger toward the dead onto the living. Deathbeds are fertile spawning grounds for family feuds—

[24] As reported in the article, "Grief: Young Spouse's Death Brings Lasting Sorrow," *USA Today*, January 8, 1984, p. 1.

sometimes the survivors get so angry at one another they don't speak until the next funeral. The feud is also a way of holding on to the departed and not accepting the death. The more central the figure (Mom, Dad), the more likely feuds seem to be. We want to blame someone for the loss, and can hate the one we decide is responsible. We fight over possessions and inheritances, not out of simple greed, but as a way of holding onto the deceased. If I can't have Mother, at least I can have her wedding china. (It's all so eighth house!)

We also want to strike out at someone—anyone—to get the rage out of our system, so we sue the doctor who somehow should have made our loved one live forever, and we rage at God for not making people immortal. Vendettas like these come out of a wish for revenge for the death, yet we cannot own up to the real object of our rage—the dead person. Many people may not experience this type of anger, yet counselors need to recognize that it may play a part in the complex of emotions that makes up grief. It can help complete the healing to acknowledge this kind of pain and allow grieving people to feel and express it. Like any emotion which is fully experienced, it transforms into something else—like love—but not working it through freezes and prolongs it.

We all know people who became embittered because of the death of someone they loved. They are angry at God, at life, at those who dare to live on and be happy. Life turns sour for them, and they themselves seem to be waiting to die. This is a Plutonian reaction which may develop from two Plutonian causes. The major one is not mourning thoroughly, resulting in displaced resentment. The more we love, the more we can also hate our loved ones for leaving us, and when we don't have permission to feel the rage, it becomes general-ized into bitterness. Likewise, the death of someone we've nursed a grudge toward also brings an upsurge of rage, along with social pressure to let go and forgive now that he or she is dead.

Secondly, even if people know how to mourn, bitterness may occur because of the lack of information about (or faith in) survival after death. How different life is when we know death is not the end! This faith comes easiest from having direct mediumistic experiences or from a medium who gives convincing evidence of survival. In this sense, a medium is a a healer of grief, and in some situations, mediums can really help. Even when we know a loved one survives, even when we have direct communication, there is still mourning and anger, just as there is with any other broken relationship, but death has lost some of its power.

Guilt Toward the Deceased

Guilt is far more acceptable than anger at the deceased, and thus far more commonly experienced, and experienced, and experienced. We feel guilty that we didn't do better by them, that we didn't call or write, that we weren't there at the end, that we didn't live up to their expectations of us—and on and on. Similar guilt can cling to the loss of a relationship or other important connection. "If only I'd. . ." Guilt and resentment are Siamese twins. So as long as we can't feel and work through the resentment, the guilt hangs in there.

Observations from Chapter Four may help people haunted by guilt about someone's death. Guilt is often related to the desire to feel we had control of the situation, that we had the power to affect its outcome by our actions or inactions. In this instance, we hold onto the illusion that if we had only done or said something different, we could have prevented the death.

An extreme example of survivor's guilt was someone I worked with in my healing practice for a few months. Her father had committed suicide, and two years later, she was still consumed with guilt. Suicide, where someone actively chooses to abandon us, seems to intensify the guilt-resentment nexus of grief. This client tortured herself daily with recriminations (if she'd only been more loving, if she'd only been there more, if she'd gone to see him that day). Her actual conduct, when she described it, was fairly devoted, but her father apparently was convinced he had cancer and chose to end his life rather than suffer. I no longer know how to reach her for permission, so her chart can't be printed here, but she had a very strong natal Pluto in the eighth, the house of death, closely squaring her Taurus Sun and Venus in the fifth house. People with the Sun in the fifth often wish to remain the indulged child forever, so the loss of a father would have been a major trauma for her even under ordinary circumstances.

Her guilt seemed related to two basic responses to death: rage at the abandonment, and a need to feel she had the power to prevent what happened. There was also evidence that she was partially mourning her floundering marriage to a domineering Plutonian (Sun conjunct Pluto). Her husband was a powerful, successful man who treated her like a child, in a chastising way rather than a loving one. She was greatly resentful underneath, but terrified to contemplate change. In anyone's life, the father's death can provoke a crisis in relationships to men and authority figures, moving us into adulthood in a new way. We aren't a little girl or a little boy any more, and we come to feel we have the right to govern our own lives, make our own decisions. With this internal growth going on, precipitated by her father's death, my client's marriage was becoming intolerable. Yet, she wanted to maintain the status quo at all costs. Thus, guilt, resentment, and grief were all bound together and kept her churning.

Our work together consisted of exploring the underlying feelings toward her father and husband, both through the chart and by discussion. We worked with meditations for guilt and resentment (see Chapter Four), making tapes she could use between sessions. She was also given several bottles of flower essences, including the Bach remedies Star of Bethlehem (aftermath of shock), Pine and Crab Apple (both for guilt), and Willow (resentment). At that time, I did not have the Pegasus remedy, Eucalyptus, for grief, or the California essence, Bleeding Heart, for painful emotional attachments, but both would have been very helpful. We also held a mediumistic session with her father, in which he asked her not to hold herself responsible but to get on with her own life. The end result of our work together was not a miracle cure, but she was able to loosen the guilt and became aware that she needed to confront the very real issues in her marriage and her own life path.

For those who are carrying guilt about someone's death, the process in the chapter on guilt and resentment, as well as the remedies listed above, would help a great deal. Survivor's guilt is common, especially in traumatic deaths and deaths of young people. We feel we should have been taken instead. Some people decide to become living human sacrifices, atoning for the other person's death by wasting their lives, perhaps becoming addicted to something. This is an extremely destructive manifestation of guilt (therefore implying a strong underlying resentment) and can be helped by the tools we have been using.

Consequences of Avoiding Grief

Grief is actually the fuel for transformation, and only by surrendering to it do we transform ourselves. Grief which is frozen is like a lump of ice in the psyche. When we don't mourn, neither do we let go of the person or situation, so a part of us is stuck there. Frozen grief freezes other things as well, like joy and the capacity to care deeply for others. Unresolved, it can easily turn into a chronic, low grade depression which saps energy. As our culture provides less and less support for bereavement, statistics on depression rise higher and higher.

It is no coincidence that as the rituals of mourning become more and more abbreviated and less and less acceptable, statistics on cancer and other such deadly diseases rise higher and higher. In studies of the psychology of cancer victims, it was found that many had suffered a deep loss or setback in the six months to two years before the onset of cancer. Doubtlessly, these people did not grieve over their losses but translated them into illness. Pluto rules both grief and degenerative diseases like cancer, and my feeling is that the rising rate of cancer in this country is not so much due to food additives and chemical pollutants as to our cultural proscription on mourning.

Transformation of the Living as a Result of a Death

Grief is a process that can't be denied, short-circuited, or sedated out of existence. It lasts about as long as the Pluto transit that ushered in the process. We must grieve fully in order to pass on to the next stage of growth. I have observed many powerful and positive transformations in people as a result of the death of someone meaningful.

This is not to negate the pain of mourning, yet often the most intense transformations follow upon the most intense pain. Perhaps with Pluto in Scorpio we will all learn the lesson of grieving, and we will all experience powerful healings as a result.

We have all seen how confrontation with even a distant death—a classmate, a neighbor's child, a media hero—can make us take life more seriously. The two Plutonian passages, birth and death, are the doorways of life, and direct experience of either can teach us more about commitment to life than any other experience. By being confronted with mortality, we determine to make the most of the years we have, and we start to work on things that hold us back. If a distant death can affect us this way, imagine how much more powerful death is near at hand. A close call with death can also have that result. In fact, the experience of Dr. Kenneth Ring, president of the International Association for Near-Death Studies, is that these near-death experiences change people dramatically for the better, giving them a new sense of opportunity and self-confidence.

The death of a parent is especially powerful in its capacity to change our lives. A number of alcoholics I worked with became sober when an alcoholic parent or even a drinking buddy died. Part of this is psychic, in that parents bind us very closely psychically, no matter how far away they are, or how determinedly we shut them out. Once a parent dies, that psychic hold is broken, so we are free to let go of their fears, neuroses and compulsions. My mother was an amateur astrologer, and I never did a chart reading without an anxiety attack until after her death. A parent's death is a painful rite of passage, yet it can free us to lead our own lives, if that has been an issue for us.

When the parent or mate is loved, the loss is considerable, and when hated, the grief/rage can be overwhelming. Most people have a hard time giving themselves permission to mourn under "hate" circumstances, because the conscious reaction is, "I'm glad the bastard's dead!" Nor do friends understand our grief when a hated parent dies. We mourn the loss of hope of ever getting what we needed; we mourn the fact that we will never be able to reconcile our differences. After all, where there is hate, most of the time, there once was love. Workers in the field of child welfare find that even severely abused children love their parents and want to be with them; they just want the abuse to stop. If we refuse to come to terms with the loss of a hated parent or mate, we can create serious problems, such as chronic depression, or a bitter, mournful outlook on life.

Having a Plutonian parent or mate removed from the scene can actually pave the way for an extremely positive transformation. Two sisters who had been incestuously abused by their alcoholic father were both very much overweight. Both lost a tremendous amount of weight beginning one year after he died. They were an entire continent apart and not in contact, yet their reactions were identical, once the threat posed by the father's existence and the psychic contamination by his bitter, disturbed personality were removed. Once the parent is no longer around to react, many people give up self-destructive behavior intended as revenge on the parent—those fail for spite patterns that some people develop. Not every one is affected in this way, but counselors should keep in mind that this is yet another kind of possible transformation.

Being a Friend to the Bereaved

There's no easily understood set of rules for how to respond to bereavement, and the disappearance of socially accepted customs make it hard to know what to do. We are so uncomfortable with death and grief that it is hard for us to be around it, so discomfort gets in the way of responding well. We are self-conscious rather than conscious of the needs of bereaved people (Pluto in Leo again). We don't want to be reminded that it could happen, will inevitably happen, to us.

People who are best at being a friend to the bereaved invariably have suffered grief themselves. Until we lose a parent or a mate, it is an abstraction, something that only happens to other people. After an important death, we understand other bereaved people better. If we haven't allowed ourselves to grieve thoroughly, it may still be hard to be around bereaved people, yet we do understand. If we let ourselves remember what our grief was like, we can share important bits of the process. (Don't go into detail about your own pain, because the person can't respond to your need when he or she is going through the mourning period.) It is very comforting when someone else says, "Yes, it would come and go for me too. Sometimes I'd almost forget about it, then all of a sudden I'd be flooded with it, as bad as the day he died. That went on for more than a year." The payoff is that we get to complete a bit more of our own mourning—a process that seems to go on for years, to a diminishing extent.

How can we help if we haven't suffered a significant death since childhood? Remember the most painful loss ever suffered (a broken relationship, a failed dream) to gain insight into the pain of grief. Plain old garden variety sensitivity and listening are the best tools. Books about grief and dying (see the bibliography) can help us understand the process of grief better. Ask how the grieving person feels. Listen. Don't talk. Touching is much better than talking; people who are grieving need the comfort of being held. If they lost a mate, they especially need to be touched because that natural part of life is gone.

Don't feel a need to supply answers, because there aren't any. Platitudes enrage bereaved people. Remember that bereaved people are full of anger at their loss, so they readily turn their anger onto the living. They may have a chip on their shoulder, so don't take it personally, turn the other cheek. And, like all Plutonian emotional states, grief can be obsessive, so be prepared to hear the same painful thoughts and feelings over and over. Some people need to do that in order to process and resolve the conflicts and emotions. It is also necessary in order to make the death real, as it is so incomprehensible.

Don't present psychological insights, metaphysical sophistry, or advice on what they should do with their lives. They don't want to hear that Charlie was really rotten, or that it was good he died so he wouldn't have to suffer any more. Maybe they will say those things, but they don't need to hear someone else say them. Just keep coming back to the fact that they are sad and you are sorry they hurt. That's all you can give them. And don't assume they are over it or that they are taking it well since they aren't talking about it any more, because there are hiatuses in mourning. They may go deeply into it six months or a year later and really need someone to listen then. It's a process that cannot be stopped without harm. It is their process and will be individual to them, depending on who they lost and all the complexities of that relationship, as well as what other losses they've had. They do not need judgements on how that process should go or when it should be over.

Finally, what can you do for your loved ones who have died? They need your love and caring too, so you might treat them as you would a good friend who has moved away and is lonely. Talk to them mentally now and then and tell them you miss them. Say all the things you would have said if you'd known that death would part you. Don't be surprised or fearful if they talk back or if you dream of them; that communication is actually as friendly and natural as any you had while they were alive. Don't be frustrated if you *don't* get an answer, however, because the dead may go into a healing sleep for some part of the first year or two.

The plane the dead live on is a mental/emotional one, possibly a part of the astral plane, so thoughts are material there. Thus, I often create flowers in my mind for my loved ones on that side. About nine months after my father died, I received a communication from him that it was Decoration Day and he wanted his grave decorated. That's how I knew it was authentic, rather than my own wishful thinking. At that point, all Memorial Day meant to me was picnics. It would not occur to me to call Memorial Day by the old-fashioned term of Decoration Day, but it certainly would be within the vocabulary and desire pattern of an old timer like my father. Since I was 1500 miles away from his grave and we had no family there, there was no way I could honor his wish, so I lovingly built a large bouquet of peonies in my mind and placed them on his grave. (That's what we did on Decoration Day in Iowa; we put peonies on the graves and then we watched the Legionnaires and Girl Scouts honor the dead in a parade.) This action seemed to satisfy my father, and it felt nice to me, too.

As for your own loved ones, they might like some of the old rituals and find them comforting. I'm not Catholic, but I've lit candles in churches for departed people. They're really not so different from living people, or from what they were like when they were alive. All they really need is to be remembered, just like any one else, so you could do something special that they liked and do it in their memory. Remember that they are astral, so it is literally the thought that counts. It's not so hard, really—it's just being a friend.

Example:
Dying with Dignity Despite It All

Many of the psychological and astrological principles we have been discussing are illustrated by Chart 18, which belongs to a young man named Philip who died of AIDS. The illness was diagnosed in April, 1984, five months before Philip's death, when a bout of

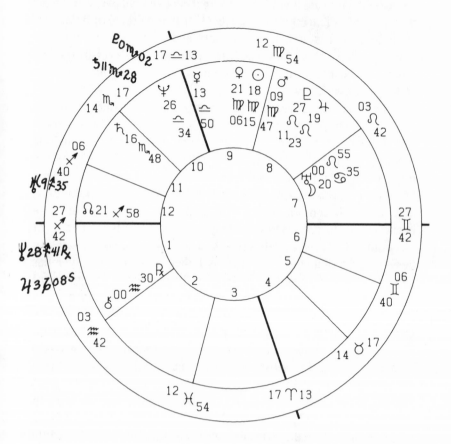

Chart 18. Philip. He died from AIDS on August 29, 1984, and the transits for the day of his death have been written around the outer circle. Birth data for his natal chart is not available for reasons of confidentiality. Chart used by permission.

pneumonia had persisted for more than a month and kept getting worse. The illness had doubtlessly been going on for some time, as there were strange and unexplained skin conditions and other symptoms. Philip and his lover had moved to the young man's home town some two years previously, and doctors there were not looking for AIDS, just as people there were not looking for homosexuality.

When the bout of pneumonia began (April 9, 1984), Saturn in Scorpio had been stationary for a while on his natal Saturn (the Saturn return). Neptune had been crossing his ascendant for several years, which might indicate a progressive weakening of his resistance, and was stationary nearly there at the time of his death. In his natal chart, Uranus sat on the cusp of his house of sex and death, and transiting Pluto had squared that several times, being fairly close at the time of death. (Natal Pluto is in the eighth house, so that both in its intrinsic meaning and in its meaning in Philip's chart, it signified a death.) Uranus had been stationary for a week or so before the death, making a very close square to Mars in the eighth house, and was on the horizon at the time of the death. While people can and do have many of these transits without coming down with AIDS, the combination of those transits plus the strong natal emphasis on the eighth house shows the possibility of his death.

I shared the last five months of Philip's life via frequent phone calls. There was never any remission, just a steady deterioration. The couple suffered a great deal of rejection and isolation from people in their circle who could not accept the implications of the illness. More love and practical assistance in his arduous nursing care came from comparative strangers, such as people in an AIDS support group. Philip's family began by denying the seriousness of the illness and hiding its true nature from others. His brother and older sister never once came to visit him in the hospital, and no one in the family gave any emotional support or help with the medical problems. Throughout the terminal illness, vengeful and vindicative things were done to Philip's lover, who was a target for the parents' resentment because Philip was gay and dying in what they perceived as a scandalous fashion. At the funeral, the parents refused to speak to Philip's lover and ordered others to do the same. They also arranged to have the electricity turned off a day or two after the funeral, since the account was in Philip's name.

It was a deeply moving experience to see this couple working through the stages of dying with a high degree of consciousness. Philip's lover had worked as a professional medium in England, and the two of them had previously studied Kabala, including those sections on death. Thus, Philip's lover was able to teach him what to expect and to help him lovingly in various stages. They were also able to talk through and resolve various difficulties that had existed in the relationship, so that the atmosphere was one of love.

As Philip died, his lover saw the Angel of Death, a towering being of light, not a frightening but a benign presence. One of his students in a psychic awareness class also saw the angel in a dream, and, in addition, received clear and specific messages from Philip, involving things only the two men knew about. In the week after the death, on August 29, 1984, numbers of people, including myself, had experiences of his continuing presence in spirit. Despite the tragic circumstances Philip and his lover, and everyone who remained close to them, grew from the experience. To die with such consciousness is rare at this point, yet Pluto in Scorpio should be an era when more and more awareness, information, and healing are available to the dying and bereaved.

Indications of Mediumistic Abilities

Mediumistic abilities take several forms. Some people have the ability to perceive or communicate with people who have died. Many people dream about having conversations with their loved ones who have died. Some people feel the physical sensations of the disease the person died from, and this is often a signal the person is around and wants to communicate. Other people, rather than communicating with people they know who have died, communicate with spirit guides. This happens quite naturally, yet often without conscious awareness, as in writing that is inspired. This latter form of mediumship is extremely common, yet not recognized by a majority of people who are helped by their guides.

In our culture, many people are mediumistic without knowing it because the church does not recognize life after death and reincarnation as well as it did in the early days of Christianity. Many world religions recognize the truth of survival after death and provide structures and rituals enhancing communication. The Spiritualist Church, for instance, began in the United States in 1848 during the Pluto/Uranus conjunction in Aries, signifying a powerful and exciting exploration. This initiated a period when seances, floating trumpets which spirits spoke through, and spirit materializations were common. Although some of these manifestations were genuine, they were exhausting for the medium to sustain, so the movement was greatly hurt by fraudulent practices. For the most part, it dwindled in the United States, yet survives in England.

English mediums, influenced by the scientific investigations of the British Society for Psychical Research, are well-trained and rigorous in their search for evidence of survival. They will not accept a vague statement which anyone could twist to have the desired meaning, but instead insist on concrete, verifiable evidence. Spiritualism also is strong in the Latin American countries, in a much more emotional form and with admixtures of practices and rituals of earlier native and African religions.

The astrological indications of mediumistic abilities have to do with a prominent Pluto, Scorpio, or the eighth house. This is in contrast to a prominent Neptune, which is more akin to clairvoyance. I've included example charts of two of England's foremost mediums, Andreas Vasilou and Mrs. Jesse Mason. As you will see, Andreas Vasilou (Chart 19 on page 146) has a strong Pluto in the sixth house. Mrs. Mason (Chart 20 on page 147) has Pluto culminating, in the most powerful spot according to the Gauguelin research. It is conjunct both the Midheaven and her Sun. The person who becomes a professional medium would be likely to have Pluto or Scorpio in the sixth or tenth, probably near an angle.

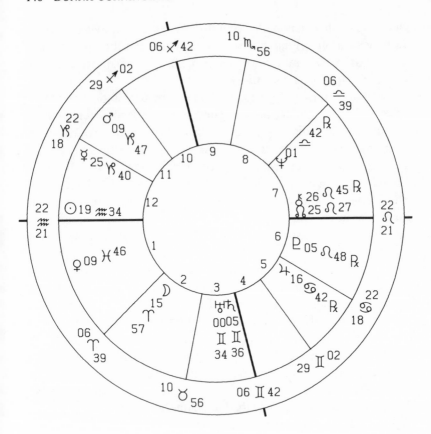

Chart 19. Andreas Vasilou, one of Europe's most famous mediums. Born Famagusta, Cyprus, February 9, 1943, at approximately 6:50 AM, tropical, Placidus. Birth was supplied to me by Vasilou; chart used by permission.

All people with Pluto prominent in their charts, however, would tend to have mediumistic abilities, whether they are conscious of having the ability or not. In fact, mediumistic tendencies may be one reason Plutonians tend to withdraw from society. Whether you develop your gift or not, it would help to be informed about what to expect and how to shield and ground yourself psychically, since any time you are around death you might experience the emotions or symptoms of the deceased or

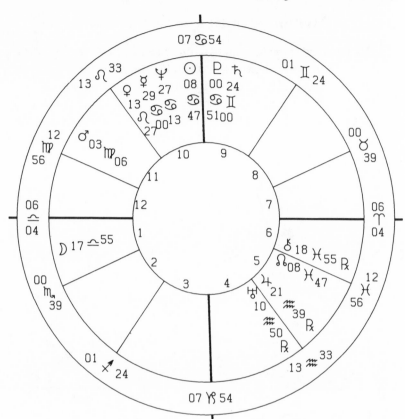

Chart 20. Mrs. Jesse Mason, a well-known medium in England for many years. Born London, England (51N31, 0W06), July 1, 1914, at noon. Data supplied to me by Mrs. Mason; chart used by permission. Mrs. Mason has since died, in December, 1984.

the survivors without being consciously aware of what is happening to you. It is important to recognize when departed people may be trying to communicate or when their emotional state may be influencing you psychically, so that you can both shield yourself and know what to do for them. An excellent book on the subject is Joey Crinita's *The Medium Touch*, listed in the bibliography.

Mediumship as a Healing Tool

As indicated at the beginning of this chapter, I am a medium, yet I only use this gift when absolutely necessary. Recently, it has become clear that mediumship is a form of healing. Sometimes, when a loss has been extremely traumatic or difficult to accept, mediumship is the only healing tool that will resolve the difficulty. Knowing that a loved one has survived beyond death can be profoundly com-

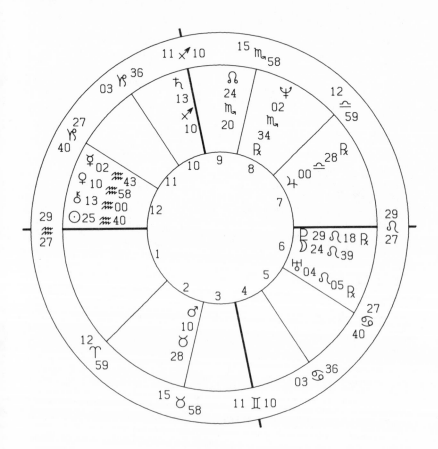

Chart 21. Linda. Born Encino, California, February 14, 1957, 6:55 AM PST, tropical, Placidus. Chart used by permission.

forting, for many people feel even more desolate when they think there is only "nothingness" afterward for the person they miss so much.

In order to better understand mediumship's healing properties and its many connections to the planet Pluto, let's look at a case example. Linda was a 25-year-old recovering alcoholic and drug abuser who belonged to my healing group. She came for an individual healing session because of her identification with a much-loved aunt who committed suicide four years earlier at a young age. Linda had felt no love coming from her alcohol-addicted parents or from her peers, so this aunt was one of the few people to whom she felt close. A near-fatal suicide attempt of her own at age 19 brought Linda into drug and alcohol treatment programs, and she has remained free of these substances since then. She works very hard at her recovery through the Anonymous programs, individual psychotherapy, and service to other addicts. Nonetheless, she continued to have suicidal desires and a deep conviction she would die as her aunt did.

Linda's chart is shown as Chart 21. She is extremely Plutonian, a pattern rather common to children of alcoholics. Pluto is precisely on the Descendant, forming a conjunction to her Moon and an opposition to her Aquarius Sun and Ascendant. People with Aquarian planets opposite Pluto are more fixedly and self-destructively rebellious than the average Aquarian, in that they are determined no one will control them the way their parents attempted to. Neptune in Scorpio, is in the eighth—a somewhat suicidal placement. This combination suggests the use of drugs as an instrument to tempt death, and also that death would be perceived as an escape. Uranus square Neptune is similar to the Aquarius/Pluto theme of rebelling at the expense of self. After studying her chart, I felt that her suicidal fantasies were something to be concerned about, as it bespeaks a desolate, Plutonian isolation.

We decided to work on Linda's identification with the aunt who committed suicide. In this case, I had no hesitation about acting as a medium, for the need was quite a valid one. I also suspected that exposure to the aftermath of suicide would dissuade Linda from acting on her own fantasies about death. We drew an imaginary circle of protection around us, and I went into trance. In the circle, the presence of the aunt, as well as her deep sorrow and remorse, were quite palpable. Linda herself was fully able to perceive her aunt's feelings. (Linda's strong Pluto indicates she had undeveloped mediumistic abilities of her own.)

We learned that the aunt's suicide was for a totally different reason than Linda's attempts; they were two entirely separate issues. Linda was gay and had opted out of the traditional female role. The aunt had married only to conform to convention; she never wanted to be a mother, but she had no conception of any options. When a child was born to her, her rage at the infant's demands and at being trapped in this role became overpowering. She finally killed herself on impulse to avoid killing the infant.

Even though her death had occurred four years earlier, it was clear that this deceased woman continued to suffer deeply with remorse. She was still tied closely to the earth plane, and part of Linda's suffering and suicidal preoccupation may well have been due to perceiving her aunt's condition mediumistically. Being a faithful Catholic and thus even more guilt-ridden because of the church's prohibition on suicide, the aunt requested that Linda go to a church and light a candle on her behalf. Linda, herself a lapsed Catholic, did this and found it comforting. (The reader should not conclude that this kind of prolonged suffering necessarily happens to all suicides—it may well be different for others.)

Although this session was definitely a "heavy," Linda was less upset by it than the average person would be, since Plutonians do not flinch at confronting hard things. It produced strong healing results. Through what we learned, Linda could separate from her identification with her aunt. More important to the healing process, she could see that suicide did not enable you to escape from an unhappy phase of your life, for she learned that it fixated you there for a longer period. Suicide ceased to be an option for her. Linda's life has been changed by her courage, for she not only faced up to her grief, but she also gained knowledge of her inherent mediumistic abilities.

Although we cannot be sure of the ultimate effects of our session on Linda's aunt, many mediums call this kind of contact "rescue work," for letting the aunt tell her story freed her so she could let go of guilt and begin to adapt more fully to her new condition. The ritual of confessing the guilty secret is a valid Plutonian healing, no matter which plane you happen to inhabit at the moment. Spirits can have a difficult time letting go of the earth plane when their death has a particularly Plutonian quality, such as suicide, murder, betrayal, or having a guilty secret. In such cases, their turmoil can be troublesome to survivors who have mediumistic tendencies, however untrained. Intervention by a trained medium can help release them.

Healing Tools for Grief Work

The best healing for mourning is mourning; there is no substitute for actively confronting your feelings about the loss. Seeking out memories, personal belongings, or favorite songs will bring on the pain, and it is important to let yourself have the grief. Others may say you should try to forget, shouldn't wallow in it, or that you are being morbid, but they are not mourning, or perhaps they can't confront their own feelings. Mourning takes time; there is no way to fast forward through it, so have patience with yourself.

The bibliography for this chapter lists a number of books. These may be be extremely helpful, but keep in mind that you may not be able to read them all at once. Since people in this culture tend to isolate those who grieve, it is a great comfort to read books by others who know exactly how you feel, to know that you are not alone in your intense and sometimes inexplicable reactions. The books about life after death and reincarnation can also be very comforting, even if you already believe in them, because now is a time when the inner, younger you needs the solace of that reminder.

Flower remedies that would be helpful in the process were mentioned earlier. Eucalyptus is a specific for grief, as is Helleborus and Hyssop (all available from Pegasus). You would want to check which ones would be right for you by a pendulum or muscle reflex test. Bleeding Heart (from California Flower Essences) is for releasing painful emotional attachments. The healing crisis for Bleeding Heart can be quite painful, so stop if too much pain comes up. If guilt and resentment are part of the picture, the familiar Bach remedies Pine and Willow are crucial. If the person who died is someone you had very negative feelings toward—such as a Plutonian parent—then see if Holly is indicated. The Bach remedy Honeysuckle, for nostalgia and letting go of the past, may be indicated at some point, yet part of the healing process involves reliving the past you shared with the person.

If guilt, resentment, or difficulty in letting go are part of the grief you need to work on, follow the exercises in Chapter Four. The exercise in Chapter Three on opening the heart center would help heal the heart wound from your loss. Healing the heart center is a kind and loving thing to do for yourself, because it cleanses the grief and prepares you for loving people around you and receiving their love in return. It is a way out of the isolation that comes with mourning.

AFFIRMATIONS FOR GRIEF

I have the strength to grieve as much as I need.

I am surrounded by loving people who understand my loss.

The love that _____ and I have continues beyond death.

Both _____ and I are surrounded by love and higher guidance as we work to accept our separation.

I bless and release _____ to his/her higher good.

Just as _____'s life contributed to my growth so does his/her death.

My grief transforms me and gives my life new meaning.

A CHANT FOR MOURNING

If you are having trouble bringing mourning up to the surface, there is a chant that would help. It is the chant for Pluto, part of a system of channeled chants for the planets. The chant for Pluto is unique in that it is *only* used for mourning, not for the other meanings of the planet.[25]

The best way to use it would be to do the chant for the Sun, to get centered, the chant for the Earth, to establish a protective boundary around yourself, and then the chant for Pluto. Do not worry about getting the sounds right. They are spelled phonetically, and if you sing them from the heart, you can't sing them wrong. First, use some of the meditative devices we have already described to get down into a deep state of consciousness. You might want to do this in front of a candle, asking your Higher Self for help in working through the grief.

The Sun Chant:

> OH HAY YAH
> OH HAY YAH
> OH HAY YAH
> OH HAY YAH
> OH.

The Earth/Moon:

> SI IDRIAH
> SI IDRIAH
> SI IDRIAH
> SI IDRIAH
> NEH HEH MAH SET.

Pluto:

> TI YAH
> TI YAH
> TI YAH
> TI YAH
> OH.

---

[25] Information about the whole series is available on tape and booklet entitled *A Solar System of Healing Chants*, by Donna Cunningham and Andrew Ramer. Order from RKM Publishing, Box 23042, Euclid, OH, 44123. Retail price $9.95 plus $1.00 for postage and handling.

If you feel strange about chanting, you aren't alone. I was reluctant and self-conscious about these chants in the beginning, yet the sounds seem to reverberate to important places in your brain and energy body. The Pluto chant seems to precipitate stored up grief, even grief that's been stored for a long while. You do not have to do them out loud for them to have an effect.

Can We—and Should We— Predict Death Astrologically?

A question that is perennially debated among astrologers is whether we should predict death. The modern consensus seems to be that we should not—it is somewhat of a taboo among astrologers to do so. When clients ask, we generally duck the question by saying that we are not fortune tellers and that this is not the sort of thing that astrology predicts well. We may also give them a song and dance about how Pluto means both death and healing, so a Pluto transit could as easily mean a healing. There is also the fear of the self-fulfilling prophecy, that if we did predict death, we might undercut the person's will to live.

When push comes to shove, the ordinary Western astrologer does not, in fact, have the technology to predict death with any precision. Yet, astrologers of other traditions can and do predict death with a high degree of accuracy. Michael Lutin tells the story of the man from India who came to him for a reading. The client began the session by saying, "In India, we go to an astrologer for three pieces of information. We want to know the date of the child's birth, the date of marriage, and the date of death. I already know my date of birth. I already know my date of marriage. So can you imagine why I am here?"

Hindu astrologers are noted for great accuracy with prediction, and although we Americans eagerly adopt anything else that works, we do not adopt these predictive techniques, and in fact frown on predictive astrology. I suspect that this has to do with our culture and its values. We ardently wish to believe in free will, often in the face of evidence that human beings function like automatons in most of their actions. Most especially, people in our culture do not wish to face up to death—we deny it will ever happen to us or anyone we love, and we bury our heads in the sand. We have difficulty discussing it with terminally ill people and in general consider it a taboo topic. It is no wonder, then, that American astrologers shrink from predicting death. We wish to shield our clients from bad news and we ourselves do not like to contemplate death, even at this remove.

However, the work of Elisabeth Kübler-Ross has shown that telling the truth to a terminally ill patient who is actively seeking the information can help them begin to work through important unresolved issues and settle their affairs. If an astrologer were able to predict death with some degree of accuracy, could that not also be a service to the client who is asking if someone they love is dying? For me, an important purpose was served by having astrological confirmation of the medical probability that my mother was dying (Pluto was opposing my Moon). This knowledge of approximate timing helped me get to work on issues in our relationship—Plutonian ones such as guilt and resentment—so that when my mother actually did die, it was not as devastating as it could have been if I hadn't actively worked these issues through. The question of predicting, or not predicting, death is a complex one, yet I believe such predictions can be helpful at times. We astrologers need to be aware that our prohibition on forecasting death may arise more out of our own difficulties in facing and accepting death, and from discomfort in giving a client potentially upsetting information, than from a genuine understanding of some clients' needs to know and face the truth.

For example, let's suppose you have a client who has the Sun and Moon in Cancer in the seventh, suggesting that the parents would be the primary love relationship. Further, suppose the client (at age thirty-five) still lives with the parents, who are in their seventies and not in good health. You note that transiting Pluto and Saturn will conjunct the Midheaven and square that Cancer Sun and Moon within the year. The probability that one or both parents would die is quite strong, and you imagine that the client's loss would be emotionally devastating.

Would it not be advisable to gently question the client to see how prepared he or she might be for such a possible event? While I might not make a precise and emphatic statement—I could, after all, be wrong—I might still tell the client that there was a possibility of losing a parent within the next year or two and it might be time to think about how it would be to live alone. A discussion of this nature is bound to be extremely upsetting to the client, so you would need to be very gentle and tentative in the prediction. Yet, if the client can't face thinking about it, you can imagine how shocking it would be when the parents' demise became a reality. Sometimes I say that I can't be entirely certain, but nonetheless the time will ultimately come when the parents will die, so it is best to begin considering it. By speaking now, I have planted the seed, providing a forum for speaking the unspeakable, and the client is becoming a little more prepared for the inevitable. Would it not be cowardly on the astrologer's part to see such a set-up and not raise the issue in some way?

Moving Right Along. . .

Maybe this is what they mean by a lingering death. Death is an endless topic, and in this long chapter, we've only skimmed the surface. We haven't space for such Plutonian kinds of death as suicide, murder, or cancer, but the negative Plutonian energy released in such circumstances can be considerable. For those who have become interested because of this discussion, or for those with a sad, personal need to know, the books in the bibliography about death, grief, and life after death will be the source of much information. If you don't succeed in finding them, look up grief in the card catalog in the public library, for there will be other books available.

When you are coping with the death of a loved one, it's best not to do it alone, but to read what others who know about the process have to tell you. That should do much to offset all the public pressure to cut off your feelings. Best of all would be a bereavement group to provide support and understanding. Similarly, grief over other kinds of losses, like the end of a marriage or the loss of a breast, can be anguish to go through, so some of the books can give you an awareness of the grief process.

Books About Grief

Brothers, Dr. Joyce. "How We Face Sorrow and Grief," *Good Housekeeping*, January, 1971 p. 33. Sometimes pop psychology has its points. If you were only going to read one thing about grief, this would do. Your local library may have this in a bound volume of magazines.

Caine, Lynne. *Widow*, Bantam, N.Y., 1975. The story of a young mother's first year of widowhood, articulately written about the stages and difficulties she went through. Very well done, and there is a sequel showing her further adjustments.

Kreis, Bernadise, and Alice Pattie. *Up From Grief: Patterns of Recovery*, Seabury Press, N.Y., 1969. A loving guide to recovering from grief, written by two widows who have worked with many other bereaved people. (Check your local library.)

Shepherd, Martin, MD. *Someone You Love Is Dying*. Charter Communications, N.Y., 1969. A guide book for family members of the terminally ill and for the bereaved. Psychological and practical considerations of the mourning period. (Check the library.)

Books About Dying and Life After Death

Crinita, Joey. *The Medium Touch: A New Approach to Mediumship*. The Donning Company, Norfolk, VA, 1982. One of the few modern how-to books on mediumship, interesting and well-written by a solidly-grounded medium. (Order from publisher, 5659 Virginia Beach Blvd., Norfolk, VA, 23502)

Ebon, Martin. *Death and Life After Death*. Signet Books, N.Y., 1977. Also wrote *The Evidence for Life after Death* (same publisher). Two popular level paperbacks reviewing numerous cases and studies about life after death. A chapter on Elisabeth Kübler-Ross's experiences with mediumship and survival.

Kübler-Ross, Elisabeth. *On Death and Dying*. Macmillan, N.Y., 1969. Pioneering work on the stages dying people and their loved ones go through in preparing for death and in mourning. She now accepts survival past death as a fact. Author of several books on dying and founder of Shanti Nilaya, a project for the terminally ill and their families. You can write to them at Box 2396, Escondido, CA 92025.

Moody, Raymond. *Life After Life*. Bantam Books, N.Y., 1980. A careful research study interviewing 150 people who died and were brought back to life, showing a remarkable consistency in their experiences. Further research and additional topics such as suicide are considered in his sequel, *Reflections on Life After Life*, Bantam Books, N.Y., 1977.

Ossis, Karlis and Haraldsson Erlender. *At the Hour of Death*. Avon Books, N.Y., 1972. Research into the deathbed experiences of over 15,000 doctors and nurses, with 35,000 dying patients. Interviews with 120 people who came back from near-death experiences.

Books About Reincarnation

Cerimara, Gina. *Many Mansions*. NAL, N.Y., 1972, and *The World Within*. Morrow, N.Y., 1957. Two excellent and readable books based on the work of Edgar Cayce, defining the principles of reincarnation and giving numerous case examples of how past lives affect this one.

Montgomery, Ruth. *A World Beyond*. Fawcett Books, N.Y., 1971. Author of numerous books on life after death and the spiritual planes. In this one, the spirit guide is Arthur Ford, a medium and an alcoholic during his lifetime whose work is discussed in the next chapter. The story of his addiction and its effects on his life after death are told in Montgomery's book.

Steiger, Brad and Loring Williams. *Other Lives*. Hawthorn Books, Inc., N.Y., 1969. Really nice for people who have just lost someone.

CHAPTER SEVEN

Transits:
If This Is Transformation,
Why Does It Hurt So Much?

This chapter might be regarded as a survival manual for Pluto transits, because we will not only discuss the difficulties and where they come from but also some healing suggestions. You may find that practically every Plutonian character trait, issue, and emotion will arise in the course of a Pluto transit to a given area of your life. When you have a Pluto aspect to a natal planet or angle by transit, you temporarily behave as though you had that aspect in your birth chart. You may find yourself obsessed with the past, resentful, brooding, deeply mournful, or withdrawn. Events involving basic eighth house issues like money, death, sex, and birth may come up. You may find power struggles going on in that area of life, where you are now suddenly surrounded by Scorpios. Oh, yes, there may very well be a transformation—what choice do you have? The purpose of this chapter is to help you understand what is going on and find ways of working with the energy of the transit rather than against it.

This is a process, as Pluto passes back and forth, direct, retrograde, and direct over an area. You can't judge what the result of the transit will be by its first crossing, which is sometimes the most intense. You judge it by its final results, two or three years down the line. People who are sensitive and aware may very well feel the transit three to five degrees in advance, on a more subtle level. Often when clients come for a reading, you see that Pluto is two degrees away so you say, "This summer you may be feeling x, y, and z." They confound you by saying, "I've already been working on that for two years." Plutonians who are progressing toward growth often say this, for they are introspective and insightful, seeming to sense in advance the direction they are heading.

"There's Got to Be a Pony Somewhere"

Although a metaphysical approach can be quite valuable, metaphysics itself seemed to become exaggerated, unrealistic, and ungrounded in the last days of Neptune in Sagittarius. I have grown particularly impatient with what I call "Wonderbread Metaphysicians," those who have absorbed enough of the pop "Power of Positive Thinking" hype to tell you that there are no bad transits, just challenges and opportunities for growth. Congratulations, you're having a Pluto transit, and this means you're going to totally transform that part of your life. This approach reminds me of the story of the optimist who goes to hell and finds himself up to his shoulders in manure. Delightedly, he dives in and starts swimming around. The pessimist stops him to ask why he's so happy, and the optimist says, "With all this manure, there's got to be a pony somewhere!"

The client who gets a reading only stressing the upbeat, transformational aspects of a Pluto transit may wind up feeling he is doing something totally wrong, because the way he's feeling doesn't match the positive, growth-oriented experience the astrologer said he was going to have. Wonderbread metaphysicians don't tell you that sometimes during that Pluto transit it may feel like you're getting a bone marrow transplant without anesthesia. They don't mention that you are probably going to find yourself obsessed with people and events from the past that you hoped you'd never have to think of again. You could find yourself mourning someone who left you ten years ago and enraged over what your first boss did ages ago. They don't say that you may wind up alienated from those you love most because they don't understand why you can't let go of these things they feel have no relevance to the present.

There *may* be a pony somewhere, but during a Pluto transit, you have to move layers and layers of manure to get to it. Part of the problem *is* the manure—most of us create a lot of it in order to hide from our emotions. A Pluto transit means you can't hide any more, but now you have all those accumulated layers of manure to deal with. You dig through the painful past in the area where you are getting a Pluto transit, purging the feelings you never faced. The dredging up, the obsessive reiteration of what happened, and the catharsis of emotions about long finished events are actually necessary to the healing, but it's no fun to do and no fun for anyone else to be around.

Very often, under a Pluto transit, current events or conditions will mirror something in the past and bring up all the feelings that didn't get handled then. In coping with what is going on today, you also have to work through that other era in order to stop repeating the patterns. Sometimes the only way to get over the pattern is to go into it intensely—getting an overdose of it. You meet the ultimate abusive lover, you get into a near-catastrophic power struggle at work, or make the ultimate mistake in that area of your life where Pluto is transiting. You do *that thing* one more time, in such a way and with such intensity that you finally become aware that it cannot go on any longer. And out of the pain which follows, you begin to do something to change it.

No, not everyone has to go this far into self-defeating behavior during a Pluto transit. For instance, a trine by transit is usually easier to integrate. Even with squares and oppositions, however, self-aware people begin working things through before going to the extreme. You will get along a lot better with the Universe if you can take a hint, learning a lesson from a small problem, rather than persisting and getting into a larger one. A chart reading done by a humanistic astrologer can forewarn you that work is needed in this area of your life if you wish to avoid difficulty. A well-grounded metaphysical approach can help you see how you are creating your problems and how you can use this opportunity to transform old unwanted patterns. The tools and suggestions for various transits can speed up the release of old emotions which have kept you stuck. Healing and therapeutic work can have a powerful impact during a Pluto transit. Your chart can show where the work would have the greatest possible effect.

What in the World Is Transformation?

People talk so much about transformation, yet it remains somewhat of an undefined term. Asked whether change and transformation are the same, a character in one of the Star Trek novels replies, "No, change is a one-dimensional alteration, alteration of form alone—say smashing a rock with a hammer and breaking it. Transformation is two-dimensional alteration, alteration of substance—turning a non-living rock into a live flower."[26] In contemplating transformation, are we so ready to turn from rocks into flowers? Or are we just becoming crushed rocks, beaten down by blow after blow? Health comes from willingness to give up the state of being a rock, solid but unreachable.

Pluto represents the rebirth process, the complete makeover we do when we reach our own personal bottom in some area of our lives. It marks those do-or-die periods when we say nevermore to deeply destructive patterns of behavior. We've had plenty of pain, but even pain we don't give up without a fight, so we hang on tightly, even as we struggle to let go. We continue to bang our head against the wall, all the while saying, "I've had enough!" Ultimately, in the process of this two-year transit, we do stop the head banging and get on with life. We are never the same, because we've purged ourselves of behavior patterns and emotions that have hampered us all our lives.

Some of us learn very, very hard in certain areas of our lives. We may need repeated transits to that area of the chart, repeated events to get us to give up that painful pattern of behavior. When I see someone who's had transit after transit to Venus, for instance, a kind of siege over a period of time, then I get the feeling some higher part of that person's self is trying to break down defenses against relating. The Pluto transit is the point at which change *must* occur; Pluto says, "It's time."

---

[26] Diane Duane, *The Wounded Sky*, Pocket Books, NY, 1983, p. 123.

Why *Does* It Hurt So Much?

Alan Watts said, "To resist change, to try to cling to life, is like holding your breath; if you persist, you kill yourself."[27] The question of why transformation hurts so much goes back to the old distinction between the personality level and the spiritual level. On the personality level, the Pluto transit may be hell to go through. On the soul level, it may be the best thing that's ever happened to you. We need to learn to see with our inner eyes, not the outer. There is a purpose for the pain, but our range of vision is very limited, especially when we are immersed in the problem. The world of appearances judges these transits and finds them bad because they hurt. We suffer from spiritual and emotional myopia, not being able to see far enough to grasp the reason for the pain or what transition it is bringing. We are heading toward health but we don't recognize the turning around. It's like having an operation; we are cutting out some diseased part of the body that has been draining our health. Right after the operation it hurts like anything, but the body is already beginning to heal. That's what Pluto is like.

I've noticed that a healing often comes when we sing "The Never Song." By that, I mean we reach a point of total despair over some long-stuck pattern and we say, "I'll NEVER be any better in this area of life. I give up." When we come to feel things will NEVER change, before you know it something happens, something has changed, and somehow we are getting better. Most likely, because we give up our efforts to control the situation and admit we're licked, we finally accept that it is out of our control, and it would take a miracle to resolve the situation. There is something in the state of total defeat which stimulates the thinking that helps us get past it.

When we finally admit defeat, we are bottoming out on the undesirable pattern, like the painful bottoming out the alcoholic goes through before being able to give up alcohol. And like the alcoholic, we have to realize we are powerless over that condition in our lives, and we have to turn it over to a power greater than ourselves. Thus both Pluto and Neptune transits put us in touch with levels of being

---

[27] Alan W. Watts, *The Wisdom of Insecurity*, Vintage Books, NY, 1951, p. 41.

beyond the human personality. As Edward Gloeggler once said, "When a man reaches the end of his rope, he comes to the beginning of God."

Much of the pain with transits is reflection not cause, not punishment but correction. It is consequence; consequence means following along with. That is, it follows along with some behavior we are engaged in which draws pain to us. We are stuck, and the Pluto transit is working to get us unstuck, but we don't want to give the behavior up. We want to hold on to that old pattern which is killing us—maybe not literally, but sometimes with Pluto it is that desperate. When we are stuck and refuse to budge, the Pluto transit is like having a tooth pulled without a sedative, including internal turmoil and outside confrontations.

Much of what's painful out there is a mirror of what's in here, and we hate to face up to what's inside that's creating our problems. As one of my alcoholic students said, "Nobody wants to read the handwriting on the wall unless their back is up against it." Under Pluto, your back is definitely up against it, you are forced to read the handwriting on the wall—and it ain't a fan letter! Pluto transits are a time of confrontation of laser beam clarity. In one of the Seth books by Jane Roberts, Seth says, "All illness is an attempt to escape from the truth." Pluto makes you see the truth, and that's part of why it hurts. The truth shall set you free—but first it will make you miserable. Yet seeing the truth and letting your actions be guided by it are part of the healing.

Much of the pain we feel is caused by our own anger at not getting our way. We are self-willed and want what we want when we want it. We believe we know what is good for us. Many times we're in pain over not getting something that would have been devastating if it had come out the way we wanted. Some people become embittered over not getting their way or not having control. I have developed a chant to help me avoid trying to force things to come out the way I want rather than what is good for me. "Thy will not my will be done, Oh Lord." It helps with my willfulness and frustration over not getting my way. The Serenity Prayer is also useful with Pluto transits: "God grant me the serenity to accept the things I cannot change, the courage to change the things I can, and the wisdom to know the difference."

The Concept of Therapeutic Isolation

Pluto transits may bring periods of what I call therapeutic isolation. In our gregarious culture, people who go off by themselves are considered weird and antisocial, but very often in a Pluto transit, solitude is the very thing that heals. It gives us a chance not to function in that old pattern, which we are now experiencing as intolerable. We decide we aren't going to do that any more, but we don't know what else to do, so we retreat. It gives us a chance to process how to behave differently, which we will do by the end of the transit. As Dr. Theodore Isaac Rubin says, "If one is sick and must withdraw, then withdrawal is not sick but healthy. To withdraw may be a sign of feeling very badly, but the withdrawal itself is only an attempt to cope with the bad feelings and to gather strength so as to be able to emerge."[28]

Time alone is especially helpful with symbiotic relationships. Particularly when someone couldn't stand to be alone and thus got into all kinds of twisted interactions involving control and power struggles, therapeutic isolation is important. People can experience that they are okay alone; they won't die if they don't have someone around all the time. If they don't have a relationship for a period of time during the Pluto transit, it is painfully lonely at first, but they get a new experience of their capacity to survive, which changes their relationships profoundly. Relationships are no longer so "life and death," but can be based on loving companionship. The lesson learned during this time is, "If I can get along without you, I have a much better chance of getting along with you."

Considering isolation from another angle, misery doesn't always love company—sometimes it hates it. There are times when it's

---

[28] Theodore Isaac Rubin, MD, *Through My Own Eyes*, Macmillan, NY, 1982, p. 22.

so painful to be with others and to suffer their lack of understanding (worst of all, their deep down indifference), that you need to be alone and lick your wounds. You may drive people away, almost on purpose, with your anger and intensity in order to be alone, because being alone is the only way you can devote sufficient attention to your own healing, without having to consider the needs of others.

During Plutonian times—during the more powerful life periods—withdrawal from society was once regarded as normal and expected. For instance, the bereaved were excused from obligations. They were expected to be apart from society for a year after the death of a loved one. Traditionally, women were considered in their "confinement" period for forty days after giving birth and were not to go out or see too many people. The merit of this was not only for physical healing, but to allow time for the needed bonding between mother and infant to develop. In many tribes, women were also isolated together when menstruating, for reasons less to do with their "uncleanness" than with their need for rest and their enhanced psychic openness at that time.

We now consider these times of therapeutic isolation archaic and unliberated, yet each had an important healing purpose. When we do not give ourselves time to regenerate and to process new stages of life, resentment and grief can build up to toxic levels. Pluto is part of everyone's chart, and thus, in order to transform our difficulties, we all need solitude to think things through. Time alone can give us guidance from our Higher Selves, and we don't always take time to receive this guidance in the course of our hectic lives. In the old days, we had retreats and monasteries. Today the average person has nothing like that and little awareness of the need for it. Today we have cancer.

If clients complain of wanting to be a recluse for a particular period of time, tell them that's not a problem, that's a solution. If you focus on past patterns during the reading, you can help your client make sense of this urge to solitude, so disapproved of in our culture. Plutonian people, on the other hand, may ordinarily have a need to be alone much of the time, and sometimes a Pluto transit will change this pattern of solitude and make it possible for them to be more comfortable in the company of others hereafter.

Pluto Transits, Power, and Empowerment

An issue that often comes up during Pluto transits is power and how we use it. Most of us are afraid of power, and justly so, as very few of us know how to use it constructively. If someone has been misusing power—giving it away in a symbiotic relationship or taking too much of it from someone else—then the Pluto transit is often the time the balance of power has to get turned around. Power struggles can result, with Plutonian manipulations and striking back—the worm turns. Sometimes we want revenge for the way the person we've given our power to has been treating us. We aren't taking responsibility for the fact that they couldn't have done those things if we'd owned our own power.

Nonetheless, people who are having an important Pluto transit often experience an increase in power, so part of the difficulty is learning how to handle it. When Pluto is transiting the Midheaven, for instance, power is involved with the career. Sometimes there is the transformative death of a significant parent figure. I once did the chart of a Freudian analyst, and seeing a recent Midheaven aspect by Pluto, I asked if someone close to her had died. She replied that Anna Freud had recently died, who was both her mentor and the leader of the psychoanalytic profession. While she felt grief, she nonetheless now felt free to develop her own work along lines she could not have while Anna was alive.

Sometimes the Pluto transit ushers in a personal transformational experience, and by taking a workshop or doing some other kind of therapy, people experience their own power in a new and wonderful way. People involved in est, for instance, often talk about empowerment, which means releasing yourself (or others) from barriers to self-expression to become as powerful as you can possibly be. "How do you do that?" I'm sure you're asking. While all the tools discussed here can help, if I had the healing tools for that specific need, I'd probably do workshops on power, not write about it! I suspect that it takes the power of a group to help us get on with empowerment. There are so many anti-empowerment forces in our society, so much counter-conditioning, especially for women, that we may need on-going encouragement to counteract them. The whole issue of power is such a difficult one that we actually need permission to explore and develop it in our present society.

Pluto and the Pregnancy Trap

There is no such thing as an accidental pregnancy. That was the conclusion I reached after five years of social work in maternity clinics. Single or married, most women who "got caught" did it accidentally on purpose. Oh, they might not have been consciously aware of doing it, but for most of them, the pregnancy served a very useful purpose. Astrologically, pregnancy and reproduction are ruled by Pluto, and many pregnancies do occur under crucial Pluto transits connected with the angles, the Moon, or planets in the fifth or eighth house. Pluto also rules hidden motivations, manipulation, revenge, power struggles, subtle efforts to control others, and possessiveness. With many of the women with "unwanted pregnancies," one or more of these Plutonian motives seemed to apply. Since awareness of such motivations would defeat the purpose of the pregnancy, the women generally repressed them and consciously only felt upset about being pregnant.

Revenge against the mother, the husband, or someone else is a frequent motivation. In one case, a mildly retarded young women lived under the domination of an older sister who constantly put her down and did not allow her to function anywhere near her capacity as an adult or as a woman. The sister, a devout Catholic with many children, had to have a hysterectomy. Several months later, my patient became pregnant. This was a neatly chosen revenge—saying, in effect, "You've never allowed me to be a woman; well now you're not a woman any more and I'm showing you that I am!" (Not all these feelings were unconscious.)

She hid the pregnancy for four months, almost managing to wait until it was too late, but the sister did find out, and after much religious conflict forced her to have an abortion. My patient gave the fetus her sister's name. Isn't it remarkable how Plutonian the situation is? It became Plutonian in a positive way, too, because through our work together, she was accepted into a vocational rehabilitation program and eventually got a job and her own apartment, and the last I heard of her, she was married. As drastic as her pregnancy was, it did serve the purpose of ending her sister's suffocating domination and of beginning a life of her own.

Another element in this situation is the Plutonian trait of one-upmanship. I often saw this in pregnancies that spread through families. One notable example involved three unmarried teenage sisters who become pregnant within months of each other. It seemed like the second was jealous of the attention showered on the first when she became pregnant, so she decided to follow suit. The third couldn't stand the attention the first two were getting, so she joined the movement. Finally, not to be outdone by her daughters, the mother (who was also unmarried) became pregnant too. Naturally, none of them were conscious of the competitive side of the situation, but it was quite clear to those who worked in the clinic.

Pregnancy can also be a way of gaining control of a situation. I observed many married women who got pregnant just as they were being pressured to go to work or to develop in some new way. "I can't; there's a baby coming." Sometimes it is the husband she seeks to control. One woman, who resented being left alone so much when her husband started going to graduate school at night, suddenly experienced a failure of a birth control method that had worked successfully for years.

The Plutonian theme of abandonment also comes in here. Many babies are conceived to prevent a marital separation: "I can't leave my wife now, sweetheart, she's pregnant." In the good old days, many babies were conceived to force a marriage. Even today women try it, but times have changed and it doesn't work. Nonetheless, it is one way to hang onto someone who's going to leave you, because you can force child support payments on them. Even if it doesn't work and you never get a dime, you have a piece of them under your control forever, and they know it.

As an idealistic young social worker, I tended to see the woman as the wronged one, seduced and abandoned. Any remaining ideals I had in that area were shattered when a private therapy client of mine was entrapped by an old girlfriend who begged him to come up for a weekend for old time's sake, assured him she was sterile, and a month later, wrote him to say, "Guess what!"

Even if this method of getting your man works, the person who is trapped into the marriage often feels extremely resentful, and will make the woman—and unfortunately, the child—pay for it. Whether it works or fails, the mother is also likely to resent the child, especially if it resembles the father. The child is often a pawn between two people embroiled in Plutonian power struggles. What happens to the child? Well, it grows up to be a Plutonian, that's all.

Michael Lutin recently observed to me that many of his clients became pregnant as Pluto left Libra, as a way of holding on to a relationship that had already died. The Pluto/Saturn conjunction happened at the end of Libra, and in doing research I found that both the Pluto/Saturn conjunction of 1982 and that of 1947-48 were accompanied by marked increases in the birth rate, perhaps for Plutonian reasons. The conjunction of 1947 ushered in the great Baby Boom, but was followed a year later by the greatest peak in the divorce rate in our country's history. Although the births may have been an attempt to avoid abandonment, it did not in fact succeed. Not coincidentally, women worked outside the home for the first time during WWI *and* WWII. When the men came home, the women were forced to give up the little bit of power they had attained. The Baby Boom was doubtlessly a response to this problem around women's power; pregnancy itself is often the ultimate weapon in the power struggle between the sexes. Keep 'em pregnant and barefoot is an old male joke (ha ha) that contains a great truth about the relationship between the sexes.

I have also seen the issue of power and pregnancy arise when women (single or married) get pregnant just at the time when they had the opportunity to move ahead in a career. One such instance at the clinic was a sweet young woman, who not only was the first in her large and very troubled family to graduate from high school, but she had also won a scholarship to college. It was sad to see her leave behind her bright hopes and become another welfare mother. Perhaps she would one day reclaim her potential, but it would be very difficult, given her background and environmental pressures. For such women, and she was only one of many, to move forward meant emotional abandonment, risking the resentment and jealousy of her family and peers, leaving them behind and moving into terrifying and lonely territory.

The risks of advancement are very clear in her case, yet all women face such risks when they dare to be powerful. Women are taught to be dependent, and movement into success is threatening to others—especially the men in their lives. Lest you think only women employ the pregnancy trap, men have been known to maneuver women into pregnancy to keep them from advancing. Many men don't deal very well with a woman's success.

Many times, when women clients are having Pluto transits to the Midheaven, they tell me they are on the verge of a promotion, or their business is just taking off, but they suddenly feel they MUST have a child, because the biological clock is running out (I've had thirty year olds tell me this). The issue, as we discuss it further, is that these women are having to face up to the fearsome issue of becoming powerful and successful, and this wonderfully acceptable feminine reason becomes their cop out so they don't have to deal with becoming powerful. My feeling is that the child conceived for such a reason, just as the mother is beginning to make good in a career she loves, is either going to be resented or will be the mother's substitute for the power she lost. (After all, that child's Pluto will forever form an aspect to the mother's Midheaven.)

By now you must be asking whether there are any nice reasons to get pregnant. Yes, two people can decide they love each other and want a child. But I've been talking about unconscious decisions made for the wrong reasons. When undertaken for the right reasons (and sometimes even when it is not), parenthood, like many other Plutonian pursuits, can be the source of transformation. I can't remember the author's name or where I read this, but the words stuck in my mind: "The miracle is not that adults produce children, but that children produce adults." The crisis of adjusting to parenthood takes about a year of hard work, so pregnancy and first year of a child's life correspond to the most intense part of a two-year Pluto transit.

Another quotation that illustrates this principle was one I found in a newspaper column, written by John Carroll of the *San Francisco Chronicle*: "I rejoiced in the transforming nature of fatherhood. The side effects of being a parent were surprising and satisfying; I perceived, for the first time, my own mortality—these beings would outlive me—and my own immortality—these beings carried, among other things, the memory of my existence within them. And their existence, and my relation to their existence, helped me to understand my own parents. Oh, yes, I said to myself, I see. Got it, Mom. Not all that easy. Yes."[29]

Pluto Transits to the Natal Chart

The Appendix lists Pluto's movements over the past ten years. The lists can alert students to past and future Pluto transits to their own charts. During a transit of Pluto to the planets in the birth chart, any number of the issues we have been discussing may come up. You may find yourself confronted with obsessive thoughts of the past, power struggles in the area of your life where the transit is operating, compulsive relationships with Plutonian people, a birth or a death. These external events are merely the manifestation of—as well as the catalyst for—the process you are going through internally. The ultimate result of that process, if you work to heal yourself, is transformation of how you operate in that area of your life. Let's look at individual transits of Pluto to natal planets.

PLUTO TO THE SUN

The process going on here is the purification of the self. Becoming intensely self-obsessed, you may first exaggerate to a painful degree, then be healed of, the negative traits of your Sun sign, as you evolve in the direction of the positives. False self-concepts are stripped away and mourned, ultimately revealing the true self. Old evaluations of self-worth, both unmeritedly negative and unmeritedly egotistical, are acted out, bringing you ultimately to a more realistic self-acceptance. Sometimes, the death of an important male figure may

---

[29] John Carrol, *San Francisco Chronicle*, August 2, 1983, p. 31.

initiate this major reformation of the identity. Power and making an impact may also become an obsession, with resentment toward those who do not validate your talents.

The California Flower Essence Sunflower is extremely useful in balancing the ego and bringing about a true self-acceptance. Their essence Sagebrush is for finding your true self by letting go of false identifications. Work to clear out the solar plexus chakra is very useful. You may do this by imagining a ball of white fire in the solar plexus, burning away self-doubt and ego problems. Lavender fire for guilt can also be useful to those afflicted with self-hate, perhaps using the Whirlpool cleanse on page 61. The exercise for opening the Heart Flower (see page 63) may be changed by imagining the flower in your solar plexus instead. Design affirmations about self-worth and self-love.

PLUTO TO THE MOON

Issues around dependency and nurturance come to the surface at this time. The relationship with the mother is closely examined, with old conflicts and resentments arising as strongly as in childhood. By obsessively analyzing and reliving them, you become ready to let them go. Patterns of symbiosis or dependency derived from the mothering you got may be acted out with key women in your life and changed, since a shift in dependency patterns is going on internally. The image of what women should be is usually also challenged, with some resentment and conflict about feminine stereotypes. There is a possibility that these changes could be triggered by the death of the mother or a key female figure. Equally often the mother herself goes through a major transformation, giving her children permission to change how they relate to the issue of femininity. Another transformational event could be parenthood, yet the pregnancy could be undertaken for manipulative reasons, such as to remain dependent or in control in a relationship, or to avoid becoming more powerful in the outside world.

Nancy Friday's book, *My Mother, My Self*, is an extremely useful one to read during this transit. (I have also written a book on the Moon called *Being a Lunar Type in a Solar World*, which would help you in exploring Moon-related issues.) Rebirthing during this period could be extremely powerful. An appropriate remedy might be the California Flower Essence Pomegranate for the healing of emotional extremes due to improper nurturing in childhood. The Bach remedy Red Clover is for the overanxious or overprotective mother.

Another likely process during this transit occurs when emotions you have been unwilling to deal with come to the surface and demand attention. They are chewed over and over, much to the discomfort of you and those nearest. There can be a catharsis of unresolved feelings about the past or of issues not dealt with in the present. There is no more hiding—the emotions are right on the surface, and you get to learn new patterns of facing and dealing with them. You are in a self-analyzing mood and may be drawn to study psychology in order to understand where these feelings come from. The result is greater emotional health and awareness, rather than repression, yet your feelings would not have been buried in the first place if you knew what to do with them, so it can be rather uncomfortable at the onset. The California Flower Essences Fuschia and Scarlet Monkeyflower are for integrating repressed emotions. Something akin to primal therapy might produce the intensive catharsis this transit calls for. This could also be an effective time for Rolfing or other body work where emotions long held in the body are released.

PLUTO TO MERCURY

Here the capacity for thinking and analyzing is deepened and you are likely to be drawn to study psychology, the occult, reincarnation, or healing. Old belief systems are challenged and you must accommodate new ideas. You may pursue these new interests obsessively, possibly finding it difficult to communicate with former intimates who do not share them. Communication in general becomes an issue—you may have a compulsion to speak up about things you once considered unspeakable, or you may have a sense of not being able to communicate at all about some important matters. Speak first through your Higher Self to the Higher Self of the other person, saying what is in your heart. Relationships with brothers and sisters may reach a point of no return, for old patterns of relating, or issues from the past must be resolved or the connection may effectively be severed.

Writing, as in journals, may be used as an emotional catharsis and a healing tool. For example, the process developed by Ira Progoff known as the Intensive Journal Workshop uses written dialogues with parts of yourself to integrate and reconcile inner dissonance. This may be a time when you develop your writing ability and have the capacity to focus on important writing, research, or study projects.

PLUTO TO VENUS

A Scorpio or other Plutonian may enter your life and you may have an intense love relationship. Alternately (or in addition) long-standing love relationships endure a crisis in which resentments and other long-hidden issues come to the surface and must be resolved. Relationships become the forum in which the issue of power is examined, and there is also the necessity of examining the sexual dimension of your relationships. Some of you may feel the need to be alone or celibate for a year or longer to break destructive relationship patterns, so that you are rather lonely. At the end of that time, however, you understand that you won't die without a relationship, so relationships are much healthier, not so compulsive.

One way healing can occur is to go back over painful broken relationships, mourning them completely, purging resentments about them, and analyzing what really happened in the situation. Regularly using the exercise to open the heart flower is powerful. California Flower Essences that would be useful are Bleeding Heart, (for releasing painful old attachments), and Mariposa Lily, Shooting Star, and Dogwood (all for receptivity to love). Pegasus and other companies sell essences based on gemstones and can provide Turquoise and Ruby, which are both good for healing the heart center. Bach remedies Honeysuckle (for letting go of the past) and Star of Bethlehem (for releasing old shocks and traumas) may be important if you've had a traumatic relationship breakup.

PLUTO TO MARS

Problems around anger and self-assertiveness now come to the surface and demand to be confronted. You ultimately transform how you deal with these issues, yet in the meantime they can become obsessive and uncomfortable. You may find yourself brooding about current situations where you have given away your power. You may also obsessively relive past situations where anger was buried, in order to experience a healing catharsis. Ultimately, you can no longer bear to be quiet when you need to assert yourself, so you learn to speak up, no matter how hard that has always been.

For you who deal with anger in an excessively aggressive way, the worm may turn, and the people who were intimidated by you in the past may begin asserting themselves, so that you have to learn to be less compulsively powerful. If anger has been dealt with destructively, old patterns can be played out in a dangerous way, so outside help is advisable. The issue of the masculine stereotype is also addressed, perhaps by confrontation with a man who forces you to reclaim your own power.

Healing can come from doing the work on resentment in Chapter Four including the exercise with the purple ball. *The Angry Book*, by Theodore Isaac Rubin, is very helpful in understanding the results of not dealing with your anger. Books and groups on self-assertiveness would be extremely beneficial. There are a number of remedies for anger in the Bach kit, including Impatiens (for impatience and irritability), Willow (for resentment), Holly (for hate), Vervain (for people who become incensed by injustices), and Cherry Plum (for those who fear that their temper may get out of control and that they may harm someone).

PLUTO TO JUPITER

This transit ushers in a crisis of faith in which you find old answers and beliefs no longer deep enough to explain life's bigger questions. For instance, you may begin to wonder why being a good little boy or girl does not produce the rewards it is supposed to. Unwise giving or generosity can backfire, and you have to learn how to give without harming yourself or others. You may also become somewhat skeptical or even cynical, with your former optimism seen as rather naive.

You may conclude that God is dead and spend the remainder of the transit trying to figure out what to believe in now. Ultimately, you start to grasp the hidden meanings of life's larger questions and you come to see that the God who is dead was the one you met in Sunday school, rather than the true deity. Your mind deepens and you start searching for your own answers, rather than blindly accepting the ones you were taught by the orthodoxy. However, the more attached you are to KNOWING and BEING RIGHT, the more painful this soul searching can be. The California Flower Essence St. John's Wort is for trust in God. Their remedy Shasta Daisy is for synthesizing information from your spiritual quest.

PLUTO TO SATURN

Where Saturn is in our charts, we tend to become rigid, with fear and insecurity crystallizing us into an inflexible structure or pattern of behavior. Just as the tough outer covering of a growing shellfish becomes too confining and must be shed, so must our structures periodically be cast off if we are to continue to grow. Since that shell represents security, we are often terrified to let go of it, and sometimes it must be pried off. Pluto is the kind of transit when that happens, whether or not we cooperate. Another issue that may come up with a Pluto/Saturn transit is authority. Some difficult and even destructive power struggles can ensue with bosses or others in authority, unless the individual learns to relate to bosses and to reality in a responsible, disciplined way. The transit is also a time of reevaluating goals and ideas about success, and change is needed to remove barriers to your success.

Some of the same solar plexus cleansings given for Pluto/Sun transits can be helpful, as you need both self-confidence and clarity about your true capabilities. Both purple (for resentment) and blue (for fear) might be useful colors to do with the Whirlpool Cleanse. Two California Flower Essences for difficulties with the father, Sunflower and Saugero, can be useful here. Goldenrod Bud (for owning your own power) is another California essence that may be relevant. If the need to dominate or control is part of the problem, the Bach remedy Vine could be important. As usual, Honeysuckle (for letting go of the past), Willow (for resentment), and Holly (for hate or the desire for revenge) may be required in a difficult conflict with power and authority.

PLUTO TO URANUS

The die-hard rebel may do just that. The rest of us, hopefully, will learn how to be an individual without having to knock heads with authority. The person who has always done everything his own way and been a law unto himself may suddenly find himself unbearably lonely, so he will begin to learn how to temper his individualism in order to allow for more intimacy. What is transformed here is the need to prove how different and how much better we are than the rest of the world. Conversely, lifelong conformists may suddenly rebel and strike out for individuality.

Work on the solar plexus may be required to learn to love and trust your individuality without having to start a revolution. The Bach remedy Vervain (for those who are incensed at injustices) may be useful here, as well as Willow (for resentment), and the California essences Saugero and Sunflower will help with conflict with the father. Also appropriate could be the California remedies Sagebrush (for being true to the self) and Mullein (for finding your own true path).

PLUTO TO NEPTUNE

At least during this era of history, the conjunction happens to all of us at about the same age as the Saturn return. It often signals the death of one's youthful idealism, destroying certain illusions and breaking down masochistic patterns in areas Neptune touches. The negative Neptunian aspects of your personality may be temporarily intensified, as you do the ultimate self-deception, the ultimate rescue job, or the ultimate masochistic action. Through this intensification, you learn that it hurts too much, that you don't want to keep on hurting yourself, and you begin to change, perhaps looking to spiritual studies for answers.

Although everyone gets this transit around the same age, it is most crucial when Neptune is an important planet in the chart. In these cases, this transit seems to be handled in one of two ways: either you go into positive expressions of Neptune such as service and spiritual development, or into negative expressions of Neptune such as drug or alcohol abuse. (In other eras, due to the eccentricity of Pluto's orbit, the conjunction happened at other ages.)

Meditation and spiritual studies are the highest use of this transit, which can usher in a great amount of soul healing for the individual. You may like to use Neptune-related Bach remedies such as Centaury (for not being victimized) and Clemantis (for dreaminess and spaciness). The California Flower Essences are more spiritually directed, generally speaking. California Poppy, for instance, can help you attune to past life abilities. Since the transit is often accompanied by a psychic awakening, Yarrow is very helpful for protection from harmful psychic influences. Star Tulip is for psychic awakening, but it should always be taken with Yarrow for shielding. Using the meditations to open your brow and crown chakras can be helpful, but it is not good to concentrate on them exclusively, as you need to be solidly grounded in the lower chakras in order to use these well.

PLUTO TO PLUTO

This is a major chance to heal your Pluto problems, whatever they may be. You will be confronting and breaking down barriers. Issues around power, control, trust, and isolation are major concerns now, the transit pushing you to solve them, perhaps through the kind of intensification of the problems we spoke of earlier. The Pluto in Leo generation is getting the square between Pluto and natal Pluto about age 42, but Pluto's orbit is very irregular and it happens later for other generations. Perhaps this generation is one which needs to confront Plutonian issues sooner, so we can save the world from destruction and heal it and ourselves.

For women, this era can signify menopause or the empty nest syndrome, which is transformational in that you need to look at other reasons for being than the traditional female role. (Whether or not you actually lived the role, the ending of menstruation creates a crisis of examining your femininity.) Men can also have an empty nest crisis and one involving the limits of their power. All of the healing tools mentioned in this book for various Plutonian issues could be used very successfully during this time.

Transits to the Angles

I am increasingly seeing the angles in the natal chart as a whole. The MC/IC axis, for instance, is not two lines but one, and the same can be said of the Ascendant/Descendant axis. As you will see in the following interpretations, they function as a unit, in which events or changes in one precipitate a corresponding adjustment in the other, as the status quo is threatened. Use whatever tools for healing that connect with the issues that arise, since these are major life realignments.

PLUTO TO THE MC/IC

During a Pluto transit to the MC/IC, a career change often necessitates a major change in residence and also means a shift in the power structure in the home life. The death of a parent, which may happen under this transit, brings about a profound change in dependency and the relationship to the past (both being aspects of the IC) and also may begin a shift in one's career or life path. The issue of power is a major part of this transit, also the roots or connection to the past. For women, pregnancy does occur under this aspect, but it is unfortunately all too often related to the wish to escape from success.

PLUTO TO THE ASCENDANT/DESCENDANT

The Ascendant is our interface with the world, showing how we characteristically project ourselves. Thus, a shift in this projection of self will bring about a corresponding change in our most intimate relationships, as signified by the Descendant. The Pluto transit may show a breaking through of barriers to intimacy, perhaps because of the therapeutic isolation discussed earlier—the pain of loneliness forcing us to be more open to true intimacy. This would also be a time when healing or therapeutic work would bring about a powerful change in relationships.

The Ascendant reflects the physical body, so a health problem may conceivably arise from accumulated resentments or other stored-up emotions. Confrontation with mortality through a health crisis in yourself or someone you love (the Descendant) may make you more open than usual to closeness; even illness itself may be for the spiritual purpose of breaking down isolation through the necessity of being taken care of. In addition, getting free of illness may require a catharsis of buried emotions, and greater emotional expressiveness in itself may open you up to more closeness.

Healing Tools:
Making Pluto Transits Easier for Yourself

There are tools we can use—torches we can light for our passage through this deep internal tunnel, if we will only reach for them. Two of them, psychology and the occult, are both Plutonian pursuits, and, if rightly used, can help us have a better understanding of ourselves, our feelings, and our self-defeating interactions with the world around us. If at any time in life psychotherapy is going to be productive, the period of a major Pluto transit indicates when we are most receptive to intervention and most inclined to introspection. Naturally, the books and tools suggested in this book can be used optimally under a Pluto transit as well.

Capitalize on your Pluto transit, and your life will be much the better for it, even if the actual process can be painful at times. If you can learn from a little nudge, rather than being clobbered, the process won't be so difficult. Work hard on the first Pluto transit to a planet; work hard in between. If you thoroughly understand your chart, you can become aware of the issues and start tackling them. Do healing work on yourself in those areas—use the tools suggested for various aspects and read the books in the various bibliographies.

My own personal approach to astrology is what I call homeopathic, particularly the principle of homeopathy that says that like cures like. If you're having Pluto transits, do Pluto things. Go through a deep analysis of what your Pluto means, or of the functioning of a planet in your birth chart which is getting a Pluto transit. Try other Plutonian forms of healing like rebirthing—it would be especially good for the Plutonian who has ambivalence about living. Therapy itself is Plutonian, of course. Maybe just as powerful in terms of timing would be going off on a retreat, taking time alone to think your life over. Joan Negus recommends that you clean your closets, garage or storerooms under Pluto transits, because the objects are loaded with meanings that link you to the past, and getting rid of them helps you to let go of the feelings and meanings attached to those objects.

Sometimes the past will literally come back to stare you in the face. I often find that clients with Pluto transits go back physically to the actual situation that caused so much pain in the first place—for instance, any number have actually moved back in with their families. Friends who are into pop psychology may think of it as a collapse into neuroticism, but sometimes it's the only thing that allows you to see the past with enough clarity to release it—to see, for instance, that the people who were so overpowering when you were younger are now getting older, maybe even feeble.

AFFIRMATIONS TO USE FOR PLUTO TRANSITS

I face the inevitable with acceptance.

I trust that as this door closes another opens.

I relinquish the past in favor of a better future.

I face the future with trust in its rightness.

I believe in my own evolution toward the higher.

I am healed of my pattern of _____.

I accept a miracle.

Beating the Post-Transformation Blues

Sri Chinmoy's words can help us understand Pluto transits: "At every moment we are dying and renewing ourselves. Each moment we see that a new consciousness, a new thought, a new hope, a new light is dawning in us. When something new dawns, at that time, we see that the old has been transformed into something higher, deeper, and more profound."[30] At their best Pluto transits can be what Richard Idemon calls a *peak experience*, a time so empowering that we break through patterns that have held us back, painfully, all our lives. Thus, Pluto transits can also be times of great joy. Nonetheless, having a breakthrough in a particular area is just the beginning of the work, like having a baby is only the beginning. People not understanding this can have a letdown afterward similar to a post partum depression. In California, when I lived there, people spoke of themselves as workshop junkies, having to go back for their fix periodically.

San Francisco psychotherapist, Sara Strand, writes about the post-transformation blues, a condition that appears to be the cosmic equivalent of casual sex:

> Because such experiences can be so intense, compelling or even otherworldly, they often result in the creation of superhuman ideals or a set of standards no one could possibly maintain. It is only when we relinquish the ideal that the truly transformed person emerges: inspired and uninspired; secure and insecure; joyous and solemn; wise and stupid; independent and dependent; imperfect still, but transformed anew again, again, and still again.[31]

It's good to know that you will have Pluto transits all your life, and that even in the afterlife, you'll keep on having opportunities to transform yourself. We seem to need to go over the same ground

---

[30] Sri Chinmoy, *Death and Reincarnation: Eternity's Voyage*, Agni Press, Jamaica, NY, 1974, p. 39.

[31] *Open Exchange*, January, 1984, p. 39.

again and again, as we get transits of one kind or another to the same areas of our charts. There is no hurry; we have forever.

Is It Possible to Predict for Pluto Transits?

I don't think we know enough to predict with precision. For every person who comes to power under a Pluto/MC transit, another will fall from grace. For every one who finds love under a Pluto/Venus transit, another will lose it. For every person reborn under a Pluto transit, another will die. For every one who comes out of isolation, forgives, and opens up under a Pluto transit, someone else will become a recluse, embittered and closed off due to betrayal and abandonment.

Perhaps a difference is one's level of spiritual awareness and insight—that's a temptingly easy answer. How out of touch are you? Do you approach or avoid self-confrontation and struggle? If Neptune is strong natally, you may deny many things, so the laser beam clarity of a Pluto transit is painful. If Pluto is strong natally, you probably aren't hiding FROM the pain but IN it. But perhaps spiritual development isn't the only thing that makes the difference. Perhaps even one as aware as you could go into negative Pluto behavior with some really tragic loss. And perhaps even a spiritual ignoramus could be ennobled under the pressure of tragedy. Past performance is no guarantee of anything.

But consciousness *is* one of the things that makes a difference, and astrology is a magnificent and powerful tool for consciousness. A chart reading can help you see the situation in a different light, can help you work with the transits rather than against them. If you are an astrologer, you can make a difference by serving as an educator. But in order to educate, you have to know about more than astrology. You have to know about psychology and all the kinds of Plutonian situations we've discussed in this book—grief, incest, domestic violence, and so on. The chapter which follows is a discussion of special counseling considerations for working with Plutonian people.

CHAPTER EIGHT

Counseling People with Pluto Problems

This chapter is meant to serve as a guide to working with Plutonian individuals. In order to ease the pain they are in, Plutonians work for transformation, so you are likely to find them among your clients. This chapter is meant not only for the astrologer, but also for the counselor who uses astrology as a diagnostic tool, so some of the remarks are more relevant to long-term work than to one-shot consultations. With Plutonians, however, the intensity of the interaction is such that even a single consultation or a yearly reading can take on some of the same characteristics as longer-term work and thus require some of the same cautions. Keep in mind the dynamics of Plutonians so you have a clear picture of their difficulties and where they come from. Here we will be exploring how those traits come to play in the counseling situation.

An Aside to the Plutonian Reader

First, a note to the Plutonian person: I *know* you are reading this, because you want to know what I have to say about you. Doubtlessly there will be things in this section that make you indignant, because you never did such things and even if you maybe did do them once or twice to your astrologer or counselor, your motives were better and higher and you just did them because you were in pain. Relax, because this is really not about you. I'm talking about those other Plutonians, the ones who aren't working on transforming themselves and have no awareness of why they behave as they do, in those compulsive, rigid, painful patterns. You are obviously heavily into transformative efforts if you bought (or borrowed) this book and read this far.

But some of those other Plutonians really need help, and so this chapter is to teach the astrologer or counselor how to help them begin the work of transforming painful Plutonian patterns. Okay? Wouldn't you rather they knew what they were doing? Remember that I'm a Plutonian myself and have probably done everything talked about in this chapter, and I've also drawn a large number of Plutonians to my counseling work.

Plutonian Defenses at Work in the Session

As an astrologer, you know you have a Plutonian client when the arms are tightly crossed over the chest and the chin juts outward in a "show me something" attitude. Plutonians (overtly or covertly) say they're not going to tell you anything, they're paying *you* to tell *them*. You will probably not get so much as a nod of confirmation when you make an observation, and when you ask if what you're saying is true, they say, "sometimes." Scorpio Ascendant people are particularly loathe to tell you that you are penetrating their defenses. If you can stay calm and non-defensive, not needing to hammer your point home, they are much more able to listen, whether or not they acknowledge you.

When it's clear that it's going that way, I shrug my shoulders and do ten minutes or so of telling them about the chart, enough to let them know that I indeed do know my stuff. (If they were referred by a friend, then you're really in trouble, because they're convinced the friend told you all about them.) We don't go for the heavy stuff right away, but gradually go into it, as the arms begin relaxing and the chin moves into a more normal position. At that point, I discuss Pluto and what it means in terms of secretiveness and lack of trust, as well as some of the Plutonian personality traits and how Plutonians got that way. By then, they see that I *do* know about them, in a way that no one outside does, and that they are accepted. This may be, for some of them, a powerful and unique experience. "You mean it's okay to discuss feelings here?" It is then suggested that a dialogue would be much more productive, and by this time, they are often more open.

But not entirely. You still should not push them to acknowledge that you are right on target or that there may be something to what you are saying about changing their patterns. A tape of the session is essential for Plutonians, because when they replay it all by themselves, they can let down their guard—you are not there to contend with—and they can be open to hearing what you have to say. Don't expect or insist on validation of your interpretations or on a commitment to change anything. That would be coming more out of your own ego and power needs, and it sets up a power struggle immediately that Plutonians are all too familiar with. You become the overwhelming, intrusive parent, snooping in their diary.

They may have to control the situation—we must sit here not there, the window must be open, I want to operate the tape recorder myself, I want this set of questions in this order. If you can do what they ask without a great deal of discomfort, why not accept this need to be in control, so they are comfortable and more receptive. They are predisposed to see everything as a struggle for control, but you can put yourself aside for that hour or two to make them comfortable. Naturally, if they are extremely rigid and demanding, you can point out that their actions in the session are exactly the sort of behavior which interferes with their relationships on the outside.

Recognize and accept that they do not trust you. Why should they? You are a stranger, an unproven commodity, and they have had repeated betrayals of trust. You doubtlessly have feet of clay—we all do, and Plutonians are master clay foot spotters. Discussing confidentiality with them—*and then honoring it*—is quite important, given the very likely presence of secrets and guilt that could be poisoning their lives. Don't take for granted that they know the session is confidential; even if they do, it is reassuring to hear and creates more openness to discussing things they might not feel free to do elsewhere. In fact, an explanation of how secrets can alienate may be helpful at some point, when you get down to the nitty gritty areas.

The Advantages and Disadvantages of Working with Plutonians

If you are dealing with a strongly negative Plutonian, you will quickly see the disadvantages of counseling them. They are guarded, mistrustful, and slow to open up. Because they have so much anger toward their overpowering parents, they could try to hook you into a power struggle, whether about fees, times, where you will meet, or most of all, about getting better. In counseling, they will doubtlessly want the kind of intense, symbiotic relationship with you as described under personality traits—if it doesn't develop, they are convinced you don't care.

They can be extremely melancholy and bitter, full of self-hate and resentment toward others. Your interpretations may add to their self-hate. "Now that I understand why I do this, why can't I change?" Their emotions and the situations they are involved in are invariably intense, so be clear and well-rested when they come. As we will discuss later in more detail, some have strong death wishes and suicide fantasies. They are fixed in their behavior, pessimistic in their outlook. They are often manipulative, knowing just what strings to pull, and will lose respect for you if you fall for the manipulations. They are also great at sizing up your Achilles heel and zinging you. You will have to choose your words carefully—Plutonians will store up every ill-considered remark you make and turn it against you in some vulnerable moment.

Plutonians want and demand intensity. Once they finally open up, they may want you to keep going for hours, discussing all their trouble areas, all the past. You do not have to fall into this. You may limit your session to what is comfortable for you and tell them to come back for others (e.g., a session on the relationship that is giving them so much pain). When the financial houses of the chart are involved in the picture, some Plutonians want more than their money's worth, but you do not have to be manipulated. ("The other astrologer I went to gave me a much longer session. As expensive as this is, I would have expected more.") It is also not a good idea to bargain with them or allow them to owe you money, as the eighth house connection means they can play games over money.

Plutonian defenses can also interfere in that healing may be perceived as being under someone else's power, so they may be stubbornly resistant, almost as though survival depended on not being controlled by anyone else. (Remember that at some point in their history, survival did!) You will also recall what we discussed about failing for spite, so Plutonians may also contrive to fail at therapy. Not only does it get your goat, but if they got better, you would abandon them. In addition, the resentment and self-hate are so poisonous that until they are tackled (by the Bach remedies Willow and Holly, for instance), Plutonians may not allow themselves any happiness.

Despite all the disadvantages, there are many rewards to working with Plutonians. They are gutsy survivors of things that would have crushed lesser people, so they take that same courage with them into the healing work. They are self-motivated people who CAN do it alone. They are deep, insightful, introspective people who do not run from self-confrontation. The deeper you go and the more you focus, the better they like it. Although they may protest loudly that you are killing them, they actually love you to go in and stir things up. Their very intensity is an advantage; the "heavier" the session, the more they think it was worth it.

Plutonians have a great untapped power to heal and regenerate themselves, which they bring to your work together. Thus, they are capable of profound transformations if you show them a path of growth. They are the people you thought you made no impact on at all (after all, they didn't say a word) who come back for another reading a year later and say, "I hated what you said, but when I played the tape over, I had to admit you were right. Since then I've turned my life around in the ways you suggested." They will work hard to change, take what you say seriously, and never let go of a goal once set. (Here that same Plutonian tendency to hold on is turned to good use.) Even their obsessive-compulsive traits have positive uses, for if your work together involves meditations, written inventories, or other exercises, they will do them over and over until they get the desired result. Dr. Maria Fagnan, a California psychologist who uses astrology, suggests that the mournfulness of Plutonians may arise from the constant death/rebirth process in their lives, as they perpetually work to transform themselves.

One final consideration is that if you are doing some sort of psychological or healing work, you are likely to be a fairly Plutonian individual yourself. Thus it is extremely important that you have a high degree of awareness of your own Plutonian traits and, where they are causing you difficulty, involvement in transformational efforts of your own will help. Otherwise, you could overtly or covertly transmit a message of hopelessness about the client's Plutonian difficulties or reinforce their more negative Plutonian viewpoints as desirable.

Likewise, unless you are fairly clear on the issue of control, you can have occasional lapses into Plutonian controllingness, insisting to the client: *You vill be transformed.* You might also get involved in negative Plutonian interactions with your client, such as power struggles or symbiotic ties. It is well to remember what J. Krishnamurti said:

> Can another, however great, help to bring about a transformation in you? If he can, you are not transformed; you are merely dominated, influenced. This influence may last a considerable time, but you are not transformed. You have been overcome; and whether you are overcome by envy or by a so-called noble influence, you are still a slave, you are not free.[32]

On the other hand, the Plutonian who has worked through a particular problem is in a powerful position to help Plutonians who have not, because of the nonjudgemental understanding of where the problem comes from, how it feels to be in it, and what it takes to get

---

[32] J. Krishnamurti, *Commentaries on Living*, Quest, Wheaton, IL, 1967, p. 117.

out. Thus, if you yourself are a Plutonian who is a counselor or astrologer, the efforts you make to be free of the Plutonian problems discussed in this book will help your clients as well.

The Power of the Astrologer

Plutonians, are first and foremost fascinated/frightened by power. Astrologers have a special power, in that their knowledge of people seems mysterious, almost supernatural. Thus you have a special capacity to affect this client, in a good or bad way, so your interpretations must focus on the metaphysical and transformative rather than the negative and judgemental. Power struggles may be especially prone to arise, since Plutonians need to defend against what they perceive as your supernatural power. Due to the overwhelming power relationships they were subjected to as children, Plutonians have a deep belief in magical powers, so even if you were to convince their conscious mind that what you are doing is not supernatural, their unconscious would still cling to the belief that it is.

In working with Plutonians, the astrologer or counselor's attitude and stance is all-important. These people rarely let anyone into their private space, so great is their alienation and lack of trust, and their conviction that they are so strange no one could accept them. You are there because of the secret knowledge of them the chart gives you. Thus what you do and say is very potent. When Plutonians experience that someone knows about their insides, their secrets, and IT'S OKAY, it can be an impactful experience that could open them up to other healing efforts. Your belief that they are okay, not weird and messed up, is crucial. Your compassionate acknowledgement that they had good and sufficient reasons for their Plutonian patterns of behavior helps them to be compassionate with themselves also.

The recognition that behavior which now causes Plutonians so much pain once helped them survive a difficult, even dangerous and hostile environment is helpful. It is useful to see that it still serves them well in certain situations, that not everyone IS to be trusted. Specifying the positive capacities that came out of their training takes the onus off it. For instance, they have an exceptional capacity to understand human motivations, seeing why people are acting the way they are, and knowing what is unspoken in a situation. (Other constructive Plutonian traits are discussed in Chapter Two.) Show them that they can use these positive and even necessary traits when they need to, but not fixedly and compulsively.

Your confidence in knowing that things can get better, that there can be another way, can offset Plutonians' own basic pessimism about themselves, people and life. If you have had problems similar to the ones you are discussing and have overcome them, it could help if you were willing to share yourself and your own transformation briefly—not in gory detail, but enough that they know you *do* understand. This makes them feel that they are like you, not alien, wrong, and judged; that there is hope for them. (It also helps them relax—they now know some of *your* secrets!) I believe in sharing myself with clients and being a person, not the neutral, mysterious Freudian. (With Scorpio Rising, Freud found safety—and control—in hiding himself. Freud, after all, was a Plutonian.)

Plutonians and the Importance of Emotional Honesty

It is important that you acknowledge your own feelings, if feelings do come up in the course of working with Plutonians. These people can be quite provocative or controlling, and it is better to say when you think this is going on, if it is making you uncomfortable. They would respect you more for not falling for the game. They will also respect and trust you more if you are honest about feelings: for instance, if they are making you angry. You will recall that one of the reasons Plutonians became secretive is that people around them as they grew up lied about how they were feeling and also tried to stop Plutonians from expressing their own emotions. A high degree of self-awareness on your own part is needed for all counseling work, but especially with Plutonians.

You can be tactful and diplomatic about expressing what you are feeling with these sensitive people—for instance, you might simply say, "I don't like it that you always come late for our sessions." If you do, you provide for them a role model of self-assertiveness and dealing with anger. If you don't, they perceive your unspoken anger and think you are being dishonest; they may also push and provoke even more to get a response. BE GENTLE, however, as Plutonians are terrified of conflict because they feel it will get out of hand, or that it means the end of the relationship. It is better to speak up sooner, before you get really angry. If need be, do the exercises for resentment when this emotion comes up, so that you can discuss the matter more clearly.

Healing Tools and Their Specific Applications to Plutonians

You would want to enquire, before you make suggestions, exactly what Plutonians have *already* done to help themselves, because you can bet they have tried to transform themselves in some way, perhaps tried one thing after another in the attempt to stop the pain they are in. Give them recognition for what they've tried so far and discuss what they did or didn't like about that form of help. This approach averts the "Why don't you. . .yes, but. . ." game, in which you suggest one thing after another, while the Plutonian grows more and more contemptuous of your lack of understanding.

Self-help books are good for Plutonians, who often want to do it themselves in the privacy of their own homes. They can focus and think deeply enough to benefit from reading self-help books, and often become interested in psychology as a result. For those with traumatic backgrounds, reading about people who share their deep dark secret has a further use, as they learn that they are not alone, that others have gone through similar experiences. This can pave the way for joining a self-help group. You might wish to read the books recommended in the bibliographies for various chapters so you can recommend helpful material, as well as getting more insight into Plutonian problems. The books about life after death can be quite transformative for those with a death wish. Metaphysical books can be quite useful for the negativity.

To a certain extent, traditional talk therapy can be a corrective experience, in that it gives Plutonians the opportunity to reveal themselves to another who has some perspective on the situation, and who listens without invalidating their keen perceptions. However, talk by itself may produce insight but not necessarily change. There has even been a study which showed that talking about anger doesn't necessarily relieve it, it may only rehearse it. To offset the isolation Plutonians feel and their guardedness against self-revelation, group therapy can be a powerful healing, yet is one solution Plutonians often have difficulty accepting. Self-help groups where people of similar experiences work with one another are possibly the most powerful group experiences.

Working with some of the healing methods in this book specifically aimed at Pluto problems could be helpful. Share some of the ideas, the affirmations, the meditations, the flower remedies or other tools—possibly even this book. You might wish to be aware that if you take Plutonians through the guided meditations, any similarity to hypnosis could threaten their need to feel in control at all times. It is also important to explain as much as you can about the tools and how they work, in order to offset an unconscious equation of healing work with power and its possible abuse.

Using Metaphysics in Astrological Sessions

Astrologers can benefit from studying and using metaphysics in their work in a number of ways. First, it counteracts the fatalistic belief that Pluto, Uranus, or Mars causes the client's problems. While this point of view has been unpopular among astrologers for a blessedly long time, we still vacillate about it, slipping back and forth in our language. In addition, many of our clients have been exposed only to pop astrology, which still warns them that Big Bad Pluto is now in their solar tenth house and this means treachery in their career. We need to constantly educate clients about the part they play in creating their own problems because of their attitudes and expectations from life, themselves, and other people.

The metaphysical approach is especially important with Plutonians who are subliminally to moderately paranoid and who want to project the cause of their difficulties onto the ubiquitous THEM. They don't trust people, they expect to be betrayed or abandoned, they KNOW the boss is out to get them. Thus, they can easily take what you say and translate it into a feeling that Pluto is out to get them. It is all too easy to play into their despair and death wish, because if they feel their natal chart or transits are too difficult this means life is always going to be this way, so why go on with it.

Given these characteristics, it is important to help clients understand how they create their own difficulties in the areas of life where Pluto falls. Using the chart to show exactly how their attitudes and expectations contribute to the difficulty can be extremely helpful in getting another perspective. Let's say Pluto is in the tenth house, and the individual had repeated self-destructive battles with bosses, which led to a trail of bitter career defeats. By transit, Saturn is coming to square Pluto, so the pattern could be about to repeat itself in an extremely confrontative form. Given this alignment, the astrologer is in a pivotal position to help the client use the transit to mature in dealings with bosses.

The metaphysical approach to this particular situation would be to explore the kinds of authority figures the client had as a child, and what remaining resentment and spitefulness come from that early experience. Point out how he or she could set up the same sort of negative interactions with bosses as he or she experienced in childhood by adopting a provocative, resentful, mistrustful attitude and perhaps getting into power struggles. The boss, seeing that the client is challenging or seething inwardly at any order, may decide that the client is a person who needs to be watched carefully, an employee who is not open, who has things up his or her sleeve, someone not to be trusted. Anywhere we have a chip on the shoulder, there will doubtlessly be someone who wants to knock it off; thus the attitude we convey begs for trouble from the boss and coworkers. Thus, thought patterns and expectations in work situations effectively set the client up to have difficulty.

The astrologer with a metaphysical approach might say that the Saturn transit to Pluto means that this is a time to grow up, to take a much more realistic, self-disciplined look at how one operates at work and to approach the boss as a mature individual. It is also a time to confront barriers one places in the way of having an impact on the world, self-destructive behaviors that keep one from having the power desired in a career. Whereas continuing in the old patterns might make this an especially hardnosed confrontation with the reality of the boss's power, real progress can be made by taking the attitude that it is time to get serious about goals and to resolve authority problems perpetuated self-destructively in the career. By changing the thought patterns and expectations that go along with Pluto in the tenth, the client has the opportunity to manifest a more powerful career.

Contrast this with the effect of the astrologer who says, "With Pluto in your tenth house, you can expect to be betrayed by bosses over and over again. In fact, with transiting Saturn making a square to that Pluto, your current boss will turn out just like the ones in the past." The client hearing this would be devastated and conclude that Pluto and karma are ganging up on him, so there's no hope for success in this lifetime. Since the astrologer has confirmed his suspicions about his current boss, he begins to scrutinize the boss's every move, maybe even eavesdropping or snooping in the files to see when the axe is going to fall. Perhaps he begins cozying up to the boss's rival or superior, thinking to save his neck. The boss notices all these maneuvers, resents the employee going over his head, and starts coming down heavy on the person.

The power struggle escalates, until just as Saturn makes that exact square, the client gets his pink slip. Bitterly, he decides it will be a cold day in hell before he trusts another boss. What could have been a learning experience in turning the pattern around becomes a final defeat. Although the astrologer was right in the prediction, practically to the day, the client doesn't go back. Who needs more bad news?

Granted few of you who are reading this would interpret charts in so negative a fashion, but no doubt all of us at times say things that buy into clients' self-defeating convictions about life. We should also be aware that clients may be reading astrology books or magazines with a deterministic point of view. Thus it is important to keep voicing metaphysical principles. You may also wish to give the client affirmations to counteract the negativity, either those in this book, some from metaphysical writings, or some that you and the client create to fit the precise situation.

The astrologer who wishes to become more aware of metaphysical principles may begin by reading some of the Seth books listed in the bibliography of Chapter Three. *The Nature of Personal Reality* is perhaps the most advanced presentation of metaphysical principles in print today. Another powerful book is Ron Smotherman's *Winning Through Enlightenment*. Lectures and classes from Religious Science, Unity, or Science of Mind not only teach the ideas, but give techniques for changing thought patterns.

Kundalini Rising:
Sex and the Single Astrologer

It doesn't matter what your Ascendant is; all too often, when you do a session with a client, you've got Kundalini rising. Have you ever had the experience of being extremely horny after—or during—a session? If so, it could very well be that while you work, the kundalini energy is rising up the spinal column and that you are actually doing healing, with or without conscious awareness. Not understanding this, you may interpret this surge of energy as primarily sexual and find yourself powerfully attracted to the client—and possibly vice versa as the kundalini energy also rises in him or her.

Traditional psychotherapy contains a prohibition against having sexual relationships with clients, and this taboo seems to be a wise one. I have met too many women who were seduced by their therapists, and without exception the experience was devastating. It is an abuse of the therapist's considerable power over the client, and, since the therapist comes to represent a parent figure on some level, it is a betrayal of trust very much like incest. Yes, the client frequently has sexual feelings and fantasies toward the therapist, but it appears to be quite destructive to live out those fantasies. In fact, recently in the state of Washington, a self-help group was formed for women who have been molested by their therapists.

Astrology is an ambiguous profession in that it is not so formal and is in the nature of a consultation rather than on-going work. Does the prohibition against sleeping with clients extend to someone you only see once and then decide you want to have a relationship with? In between is the relationship of student to teacher. When a class is small, intimate, and self-revelatory, feelings of closeness can grow up which beg to be taken further. Nonetheless, if you are teaching such a cosmic, transformative subject as astrology, you as an individual get submerged in the power and excitement of what you are imparting, so your students may be moved by that power rather than seeing you as a real person. (What do I think? Well, I wouldn't, ahem, take a position.)

During a one-shot reading, it's tempting to get to know this magnetic, intense Plutonian individual sitting in front of you. The session has been so powerful, so intimate, and you really felt connected, like you were making an impact. Although Plutonians can radiate sexual energy, it would seem to be a very bad idea to become involved with your Plutonian client, considering the Plutonian modus operandi in relationships. Maybe it wouldn't be so bad to have a fling with a Uranian client—if you can handle the fact that he or she is going to love you and leave you—but it could be a terrible disservice to a Plutonian, and after all, aren't you there to serve?

For one thing, your session may have been the most powerful experience of sharing and intimacy the Plutonian client has had in a long time, but many have trouble with intimacy unless it is sexual. Sex can be used to create distance, to disarm you so that your knowledge is harmless. As we learned earlier, sex is often about power rather than about intimacy or lust, so by being involved that way, the client controls the situation and you lose your transformative power. (If you, yourself, are a Plutonian, you should also check out your own reasons for wanting to turn the emotional intimacy of the session into physical intimacy.)

For many Plutonians, all closeness has become sexualized, perhaps due to unfortunate early exposure, such as incest or child molestation. They can be seductive, but some part of them will be outraged if you, of all people, do not understand and if you treat them as sex objects the way the world does. Even if you do nothing except let yourself feel the attraction, it still can be regarded as a betrayal of trust. Plutonians are so sensitive to subtleties of body language and nuance that your thoughts are as real in the interaction as anything overt. As the kundalini rises during the session, let yourself know that it is healing energy you want, not sexual energy, and ask your Higher Self for help. A simple prayer or affirmation will transmute it.

I'd like to take the opportunity to discuss something never mentioned in teachings about healing. I and other healers notice that when you are just beginning to work with healing tools, there seems to be a period of time when your libido is dampened. This apparently comes about because the healing energy partially travels through the sexual chakra. Not knowing this, you may conclude that there is something wrong with you sexually, that you have gotten frigid or impotent. One of my colleagues was ready to go through a very expensive course of sex therapy when this happened to him, except that we fortunately discussed this phenomenon. The exercise for opening the heart chakra (see page 63) can be used on any of the chakras. If you repeat it with the sexual (sacral) chakra, located two inches below the navel, you may find it helpful in situations like this.

Counseling Suicidal People and Other Severe Problems

You need to be aware that some Plutonians have extremely destructive and even dangerous behavior patterns, such as active suicidal tendencies or involvements in sadomasochistic relationships. You also need to be aware that Plutonians are extremely gifted at covering up their trouble spots, so that you may get only the faintest hint that anything out of the ordinary is going on. To be a good counselor, you also need to be a good detective, finding clues in the smallest bit of body language, the slightest change of intonation, and most of all, in what is NOT said or is conspicuous by its absence. Being a Plutonian yourself is a good preparation for this sort of detection.

My first word of advice to astrologers on counseling actively suicidal Plutonians is: DON'T. You are over your head; for these kinds of people, you really need to know your local mental health resources, particularly the nearest suicide hot line. It would also be important to have a connection with a therapist, preferably a psychiatrist, whom you can turn to in an emergency. If you do anything else you are responding to your own need to feel powerful and in control. You may very well get the highly seductive line of, "But I don't want to go to anyone else. You are the only one who understands."

It is well known that many suicide threats and gestures are manipulations. This can be true, but you should be aware that suicidal Plutonians have nothing to lose. Either the other person will do what they want, so they have control, or if they succeed in their attempt, they will get what they've wanted all their life—death. (Read once more the section on Plutonians and the death wish.)

When you are counseling highly Plutonian individuals under very rough transits, especially Pluto transits, you may need to enquire whether they are suicidal. The average person would be freaked out by such an enquiry, but not Plutonians. For them, death is the stuff life is made of. All the same, a gentle approach is needed. "Have you ever wished you weren't alive?" may open it up. If they admit to this, "How strong is that wish? Have you, for instance, ever felt suicidal?" If they admit to this, ask, "Where do you stand with that wish at this time?" (Many have studied life after death, reincarnation, and karma—studies which are unintentionally transformational in that they come to see that suicide would not be an escape from the difficulty.) Finally, with anyone who is contemplating suicide or violence, it is helpful to get specific. Do you have a method in mind? Do you have the method available? Do you have a plan of how you would go about this? Do you have a date and time in mind? The more specific the answers, the higher the risk that they will actually carry out their plan.

Be alert also to events in their lives that might increase the possibility of suicide, such as the loss of the one symbiotic relationship, or any event that brings a great increase of guilt, resentment, or grief. For instance, studies show that men who have recently lost their mothers are much more prone to suicide. It is probably not good to predict to them that they might commit suicide, because that so hooks into their own fear/wish that it can be a self-fulfilling prophecy. However, you might note times when they would be more depressed or under more strain due to Pluto transits, and therefore might have a special need for therapeutic support.

You may be wondering if there are some definite indications in the chart for suicide. Some years ago an extensive study was conducted by the Research Committee of the New York chapter of the National Council for Geocosmic Research. A number of very well qualified professional astrologers (myself included) worked with pairs of charts (one suicide and one nonsuicide, with no indication of which was which), using both the natal chart and transits or progressions to see if it was possible to guess which was the suicide. None of us did very well at it, fortunately or unfortunately. When faced with difficult transits to Pluto or the eighth house, your best bet is to ask the client.

The Bach flower remedy Cherry Plum is useful for suicide wishes or a feeling that one may harm someone else. The Bach combination known as Rescue Remedy is available in many health food stores and is a general remedy for crisis which all astrologers and counselors should have on hand. Willow or Holly might be helpful in removing underlying hate/self-hate, but you have to be careful in when you apply them as the resulting healing crisis could tip the balance. It is much better to have your clients under professional care, using Rescue Remedy until the threat retreats, and only then to use Holly and Willow if the pendulum or other diagnostic test says it is appropriate.

In assessing the likelihood of violence, the same need for specific information exists. In dealing with an explosive marital situation, for example, you would want to ask whether battering had ever occurred, if it has been escalating, or if the partner had ever done violence to anyone else. Again you would want to know the resources for battered wives or children. If you are dealing with clients who are considering harming someone else, you'd want to know specifically if they have a plan in mind, if they have chosen a weapon, if the weapon is available, if they have a definite time or date they plan to do this, if they have already tried to harm this individual, or if they have harmed anyone else in the past. As in the questions about suicide, the more specific the answers and the firmer the plan, the greater the danger that violence will actually occur. Rescue Remedy, again, is something to have on hand, and Cherry Plum has proven useful for the person with a violent temper.

Plutonians and the Issue of Separation

First, I would have to say that traditional psychotherapy itself has a peculiar set of beliefs and mores about separation. For instance, if I, as a social worker, developed a positive working relationship with a client which was producing results, I was expected to cut it off entirely and forever if I left the agency or if the client moved outside our boundary lines—like I was dead or they were dead. Numbers of such psychotherapeutic traditions come from the Freudian model and are held as gospel, yet, as we've seen, Freud himself was extremely Plutonian where relationships were concerned. Thus, we can suppose he had more than his share of problems with separation and the issue of abandonment, like cutting people out of his life if they left him. I myself have very loving and supportive relationships with people who have finished therapy with me, yet I always feel that perhaps I am not being therapeutically correct, not the neutral totally nonself-revealing Freudian—not, when it comes down to it, as Plutonian as Freud himself.

These therapeutic considerations aside, Plutonians have special problems around separation from their counselors, since abandonment is a major issue. Very often, a crucial abandonment or the continual threat of it was part of what made them Plutonians in the first place. They've trusted you, opened up to you in a way they do not ordinarily do, so for you to leave them can strike very deep and be very painful even though they will not admit it. They're the kind who abruptly decide in mid-July to terminate therapy, denying the therapist's August vacation has anything to do with it, and denying any anger at the separation. Most Plutonians, in any kind of relationship, will leave first before they allow themselves to be left.

Although Plutonians often refuse to admit the intensity of the attachment, unless the separation is handled properly (or sometimes even if the separation is handled properly), they may very well refuse to see another counselor or astrologer. For them, it can be simply too difficult to go through the process of opening up to still another person, learning to trust, and telling all their painful secrets. If you are an astrologer who has formed a relationship with a Plutonian client over time, you may very well wish to offer the person the option of telephone consultations if you or they move away. Counselors, also, if you can lay the ghost of Freud to rest, why not let the miracles of modern telecommunication allow you to reach out and touch someone?

APPENDIX

Help For The Beginner

Getting and Reading Your Own Chart

This section is meant to be helpful to the novice or student who finds some of the explanations we've discussed too technical. If you do not already have your own chart, the best suggestion would be to get one from a reputable computer firm, as that would give you accurate mathematical calculations. It costs about $3 to have the chart done without an interpretation. You would want to consult the companies about the cost of other services, such as a printout of transits. The following companies are known to be reliable and accurate:

Astro Computing Services
Box 16297
San Diego, CA 92116

Astro Numeric Services
Box 1020
El Cerrito, CA 94530

Astro-Graphics Services
Box 28
Orleans, MA 02653

Once you have your chart, it may be hard to read if you are not used to the symbols, numbers, and layout. The first thing you need to be familiar with are the twelve houses and where they are located on the wheel. Figure 1 on page 208 shows you the order of the houses. You should also be familiar with the meanings of the houses. Keywords for the symbolism of each house is as follows:

First house: first approach to situations; personal appearance
Second house: money and how you handle it; values; resources

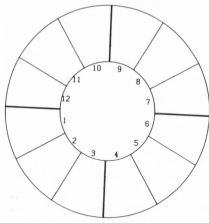

Figure 1. The houses.

Third house: thinking, learning; communication, siblings
Fourth house: the home; past; family influence; nurturing
Fifth house: children; creativity; recreation; romance
Sixth house: work and your attitudes toward it; health
Seventh house: marriage and other committed relationships
Eighth house: sex; reproduction; death; healing
Ninth house: religion; philosophy of life; higher education
Tenth house: career; your status in the world; authority
Eleventh house: friends; groups; social change
Twelfth house: the unconscious; secret behavior; spirituality

The first thing to do is to look at your own chart to determine your Pluto's house placement. Look also for its sign and degree. In some computer charts, it is written as PL 23LE14, which translates to Pluto at 23 degrees, 14 minutes of Leo. (Your own Pluto, of course, would be different.) Now take a look at Table 1 on pages 209 through 211. Table 1 shows the symbols and meanings of the signs, planets, and the houses. Each planet "rules" a sign, and the table shows you that the sign of Aries is ruled by Mars, and Aries also relates to the first house—and so on.

Table 1. The general characteristics of the signs and their connections with the planets and houses.

SIGN	PLANET	HOUSE CONNECTION
Aries: Aggressive, very competitive, sexual, strong on initiative. Symbol: ♈	*Mars:* Anger, aggression, self-assertiveness, energy, and sexuality. Symbol: ♂	*First House:* Your first approach to situations, the outer personality, physical appearance.
Taurus: Down to earth, practical, concerned with money and material goods, stable and serene, can be conservative. Symbol: ♉	*Venus:* Also ruler of Libra, here in its more sensuous, luxury loving side. Symbol: ♀	*Second House:* Money and how you manage it, your personal resources, values.
Gemini: A verbal, communicative sign, very mental, and interested in learning. Symbol: ♊	*Mercury:* Communication, thinking, writing, learning and perception, use of the hands. Symbol: ☿	*Third House:* Your thinking and communicating, how you learn basic skills; siblings and near relatives.
Cancer: Emotions, security, and family very important. Either very motherly or very attached to the mother; the past, and menstrual cycle. Symbol: ♋	*The Moon:* The mother, dependency, security, emotions, the unconscious, habits, the breasts, stomach, and tradition. Symbol: ☽	*Fourth House:* The nurturing part of your parents, effect of past family and heredity, your home life, the foundation of your security.
Leo: Wants to be the center of attention, can be egotistical, self-centered, dramatic, proud, dignified, wants to rule. Symbol: ♌	*The Sun:* The center of your being, the self, ego. Symbol: ☉	*Fifth House:* Children, romance creativity, leisure activities.

Table 1. The general characteristics of the signs and their connections with the planets and houses (cont.)

SIGN	PLANET	HOUSE CONNECTION
Virgo: Very work-oriented, critical, analytical, practical, wants to be useful, perfectionist, suffers from low self-esteem. Symbol: ♍	*Mercury:* Rules both Gemini and Virgo. Symbol: ☿	*Sixth House:* Work and how you function as an employee, health, the lower classes, often self effacing.
Libra: Much concerned with romance and relationships, so sometimes resorts to people-pleasing. Has trouble with self-assertiveness. Symbol: ♎	*Venus:* Relationships, what you do to earn love, conditions you set up for love. Sharing and appreciation of beauty, cooperation. Symbol: ♀	*Seventh House:* Long term and committed relationships as well as open enemies. What we look for in others to make up for lacks in ourselves. Who we attract.
Scorpio: A sign much concerned with power and control, can be either healing or destructive, intense, everything life or death, very concerned with sexuality, emotional but controlled about it. Symbol: ♏	*Pluto:* Control and manipulation, power, death and rebirth or transformation from one level to another, psychology, healing, sexuality, the power relations between the sexes. Symbol: ♇	*Eighth House:* Sex, death, birth regeneration, healing, the partner's possessions.
Sagittarius: Concerned with knowledge and its dissemination, philosophical, can be preachy. Optimistic, expansive. Symbol: ♐	*Jupiter:* The search for wisdom, growth, expansion, philosophy, luck, overindulgence, overconfidence. Symbol: ♃	*Ninth House:* Higher education, your philosophy of life, distant travel, law, foreign countries.

Table 1: The general characteristics of the signs and their connections with the planets and houses (cont.)

SIGN	PLANET	HOUSE CONNECTION
Capricorn: A cautious, hard working, perfectionistic sign. High goals; want to achieve, can be depressive if not accomplishing things. May be a late bloomer, serious, professional. Symbol: ♑	*Saturn:* Self-discipline, concern for quality, accomplishing things and doing things the right way, restrictions and delays, makes you start over if your foundations weren't solid, authority, fears, melancholy. Symbol: ♄	*Tenth House:* Career, status, accomplishments, authority, and how you deal with it, including your parents as authority figures.
Aquarius: A non-conforming and often rebellious sign. Can be overly detached and logical rather than deal with emotions, modern, visionary. Symbol: ♒	*Uranus:* Rebellion and nonconformity, the quest for freedom, leading to genius, inventiveness and/or eccentricity, detachment and scientific thought, astrology. Symbol: ♅	*Eleventh House:* Friendship, group membership. Social change, hopes and ambitions, peer groups. Astrology.
Pisces: Can be escapist or highly spiritual, wishes to serve others but can be masochistic about it. Can be delusive or visionary but has difficulty dealing with the here and now. Symbol: ♓	*Neptune:* The urge to transcend reality through merging with something greater—can be spiritual or escapist and addictive, hazy, can deceive self and others, what we become a slave to. Symbol: ♆	*Twelfth House:* The unconscious, what is repressed or secret which comes out in self-destructive ways. The spiritual quest, the desire to serve others, the wish to be secluded and hidden.

You might want to make a list in numerical order of your planets, ignoring the sign at first for convenience in locating aspects. For example, let's suppose you have VE 1SC12, MA 5PI57, and MO 8TA11. They would be written in numerical order rather than in sign order, because it would be easier to find the angles called *aspects* they form to one another. You might suspect, in fact, that the three listed above do have some connection to one another. In order to check out this supposition, go next to Table 2 to find out what kind of angle they might make. You would also need to see if they are close enough to an exact angle to count as an aspect. The amount of allowable leeway or *orb* is also shown in the table. You could count how many signs apart two signs are by using the order in Table 1, remembering that the zodiac is a circle, in which Pisces is followed by Aries. Using this table, you would discover that Venus in this example makes a trine to Mars and an opposition to the Moon.

Do not count the houses between two planets in your chart, as houses are of all different sizes, while the signs are a uniform 30 degrees each. In fact, as you look at certain charts, you might think that two of the signs were missing because they do not appear on the line along the edge or *cusp* of any of the houses. The signs are there; it is simply that house and its opposite one are more than 30 degrees wide. This is called an interception, and it is for that reason that counting houses to find aspects does not work.

It is not necessary for you to find all the aspects in your entire chart by this method unless it pleases you, because the main thing we are working with in this book are your Pluto aspects. In order to make it

TABLE 2. Aspects and their Allowable Orbs

ASPECT	KIND OF ANGLE	ALLOWABLE ORB
Conjunction	0 degrees apart	8 degrees either side
Sextile	60 degrees, 2 signs	3 degrees either side
Square	90 degrees, 3 signs	5 degrees either side
Trine	120 degrees, 4 signs	5 degrees either side
Opposition	180 degrees, 6 signs	8 degrees either side

TABLE 3. Finding Possible Pluto Aspects

PLUTO IN	SQUARE TO	OPPOSITE	TRINE TO
Cancer	Aries, Libra	Capricorn	Scorpio, Pisces
Leo	Taurus, Scorpio	Aquarius	Sagittarius, Aries
Virgo	Gemini, Sagittarius	Pisces	Capricorn, Taurus
Libra	Cancer, Capricorn	Aries	Aquarius, Gemini
Scorpio	Leo, Aquarius	Taurus	Pisces, Cancer

easier to read the chart, Table 3 is a cheat sheet for quickly finding aspects to Pluto in the various signs, from Cancer to Scorpio. You can use this to work with either your birth chart or your transits, which are described later. For example, let's suppose you had PL 2LE50 (Pluto at 2 Leo 50). You also see that you have SU 5AR15 (Sun at 5 Aries 15). Looking in Table 4 under Pluto in Leo, you find that Aries is trine to Leo. Looking at Table 2, you see that a trine has a 5 degree allowable orb. Since the Sun and Pluto are only 3 degrees from the exact trine, you would count this as an aspect in your chart. If, however, the Sun were at 15 Aries instead, it would be too far away from the trine to Pluto to be counted.

Another thing to understand about Chapter One is that the readings are listed in a particular order. Since the house placement of Pluto is a major consideration, the readings are done by house placement order, together with signs or aspects that have similar meanings, as already familiar from Table 1. Once you have made a list of your Pluto aspects, in order to find the readings that go along with them, you would rearrange the order of the list to correspond with the order of the book. Table 4 (on page 214) shows you those correspondences. Thus, if you had a Mercury/Pluto aspect, you would look at the reading given in Chapter One under Mercury in the Third. If you had the Moon in Scorpio, you would look at the reading given under Pluto in the Fifth House, and so on. (In the Chapter, special readings for Mars/Pluto aspects or Mars in Scorpio are given right after Pluto in the first house, and Sun/Pluto after Pluto in the fifth.)

TABLE 4. Pluto's Correspondences*

HOUSE	CORRESPONDS TO
Pluto in 1	Scorpio Rising, Pluto aspects to the Ascendant
Pluto in 2	Scorpio on 2
Pluto in 3	Scorpio on 3, Mercury in Scorpio, Mercury/Pluto aspects
Pluto in 4	Scorpio on 4, Moon in Scorpio, Moon/Pluto aspects
Pluto in 5	Scorpio on 5, (Sun in Scorpio), (Sun/Pluto aspects)
Pluto in 6	Scorpio on 6
Pluto in 7	Scorpio on 7, Venus in Scorpio, Venus/Pluto aspects
Pluto in 8	Scorpio on 8
Pluto in 9	Scorpio on 9, Jupiter in Scorpio, Jupiter/Pluto aspects
Pluto in 10	Scorpio on 10, Saturn in Scorpio, Saturn/Pluto aspects
Pluto in 11	Scorpio on 11, (Uranus/Pluto aspects)
Pluto in 12	Scorpio on 12, (Neptune in Scorpio)

* Correspondences in parentheses are weaker or else have significant themes of their own not covered by this correspondence. Where certain correspondences would logically hold, yet do not according to my experience, they are left out intentionally (e.g., Pluto/Mars aspects do not correspond with Pluto in the first). Thus, some of the lines contain only one correspondence.

Finding Your Pluto Transits

In order to use Chapter Seven, you would need to be able to find Pluto transits that you are having or have had in the past. Table 5 (on page 216) shows Pluto's movements from 1975 to 1990. You would match the significant numbers on your chart with the numbers in the first column of the table. For example, if Pluto is at 21 Scorpio and you have a planet within a degree or two of that, you would have a conjunction by transit, a very powerful combination where Pluto transits are concerned. If you have a planet at 21 Leo or 21 Aquarius, you would have a square or 90 degree angle, a somewhat difficult influence. If you have a planet at 21 Taurus, then by transit you would have an opposition, a somewhat difficult angle in which you would need to learn balance and perspective. If you have a planet a degree or two from 21 Cancer or 21 Pisces, the transit would be a trine, still requiring you to integrate Pluto with the planet in question, yet probably not in such a stressful way. In addition to the planets, you would want to check for aspects to your Ascendant/Descendant axis and your MC/IC axis, as they are also activated by transit, often correlating with powerful changes in the life circumstances.

Another thing you may find interesting is to plot the course of Pluto through your chart by transit. It does move slowly, yet when it changes from one house to the next, there is often a corresponding shift in emphasis. For instance, if it were going through your sixth house, the Plutonian events and transformations might focus in the area of work or health. At the point in time when it moved into the seventh, the focus of these energies would shift over into relationships. (Figure 1, on page 208, would help you see the meanings of the various houses.) Other than the Ascendant (first house), IC (fourth house), Descendant (seventh house), and MC or Midheaven (tenth house), the dividing lines between the houses (called *cusps*) do not correspond to events when they are transited, yet they mark the end of one house and the beginning of another. For instance, if the cusp of your second house is 3 Scorpio, Pluto would move into the second house as it moves up to 3 Scorpio, so you would see a shift into second house concerns, such as finances.

As you will see, Pluto seems to move back and forth over the same spot for two or three years. It is not, of course, that Pluto moves backward and forward, but from the point of view of the earth, it seems to do so. That is because the earth races around the Sun in one year, moving 360 degrees while Pluto is moving only 3 or 4 degrees in its 248 year orbit around the Sun. When we are on the opposite side of the Sun from Pluto, it appears to be moving backwards (or *retrograde*). When you look at a day-by-day table of the planets' motions (called an *ephemeris*), you would at times see the planet moving backwards, noted by the mark R. There are various theories as to the meaning of retrograde planets, some saying that they are more internal, but this has not been shown to my satisfaction—Pluto is pretty internal to begin with.

It would be useful to make a list of all Pluto transits you may have had over the past few years as well, but remember that other

TABLE 5. Pluto's Movements 1975–1990

YEAR	PLUTO	SQUARES	OPPOSITE	TRINES
1975	6-11 Libra	Cancer, Capricorn	Aries	Gemini, Aquarius
1976	9-14 Libra	Cancer, Capricorn	Aries	Gemini, Aquarius
1977	11-16 Libra	Cancer, Capricorn	Aries	Gemini, Aquarius
1978	13-19 Libra	Cancer, Capricorn	Aries	Gemini, Aquarius
1979	16-21 Libra	Cancer, Capricorn	Aries	Gemini, Aquarius
1980	18-24 Libra	Cancer, Capricorn	Aries	Gemini, Aquarius
1981	21-26 Libra	Cancer, Capricorn	Aries	Gemini, Aquarius
1982	24-29 Libra	Cancer, Capricorn	Aries	Gemini, Aquarius
1983	26 Libra to 1 Scorpio*	Cancer-Capricorn & Leo-Aquarius	Aries , Taurus	Gemini-Aquarius & Cancer-Pisces
1984	29 Libra to 4 Scorpio	Cancer-Capricorn & Leo-Aquarius	Aries , Taurus	Gemini-Aquarius & Cancer-Pisces
1985	1-6 Scorpio	Leo, Aquarius	Taurus	Cancer, Pisces
1986	4-9 Scorpio	Leo, Aquarius	Taurus	Cancer, Pisces
1987	7-11 Scorpio	Leo, Aquarius	Taurus	Cancer, Pisces
1988	9-14 Scorpio	Leo, Aquarius	Taurus	Cancer, Pisces
1989	12-17 Scorpio	Leo, Aquarius	Taurus	Cancer, Pisces
1990	14-19 Scorpio	Leo, Aquarius	Taurus	Cancer, Pisces

* In 1983, Pluto moved from 26 Libra to 1 Scorpio. It was square to 26, 27, 28, and 29 degrees of both Cancer and Capricorn as well as 0 and 1 degree of Leo and Aquarius. It was opposite 26, 27, 28, and 29 degrees of Aries as well as 0 and 1 degree of Taurus. It was trine 26, 27, 28, and 29 degrees of Gemini and Aquarius, and to 0 and 1 degree of Cancer and Pisces.

transiting planets may be involved in the picture too. For example, during parts of 1982 and 1983, Pluto and Saturn were standing together, an extremely stressful combination which only happens once each 33 years—this time, in the last few degrees of Libra. Thus, if you had planets in range of that conjunction, it would not be fair to judge the effect of a Pluto transit by what may have transpired then. Even if you pinpoint a past Pluto transit to a planet in your chart as quite a difficult time in your life, know also that you are not the same person now as you were then, that you may have learned a great deal from the transit. In addition, the exercises in the book should help you take care of your difficult Pluto patterns. Thus a future Pluto transit need not be so stressful.

A Suggested Bibliography for the Beginner

If this book has led you to discover what a fascinating subject astrology can be, the following list of books is a starter in learning more about this complex and helpful subject. Astrology has grown by leaps and bounds since the late 1960s, incorporating into its ancient underpinnings the culture's growth through the Human Potential Movement and spiritual and metaphysical studies. Several of the authors on the list have written more than one book. Additional authors for the reader to know about, on a slightly more advanced level, are Rob Hand, Liz Greene, Stephen Arroyo, and Dane Rudhyar.

Cunningham, Donna. *An Astrological Guide to Self-Awareness*, CRCS Publishing, Reno, NV, 1978. Yes, it is MY book, but it's still a basic orientation to the psychological meanings of the planets, houses, and other facets of astrology.

Kempton-Smith, Debbie. *Secrets From a Stargazer's Notebook*, Bantam, NY, 1982. A painless introduction to many facets of astrology for the novice who is ready to tackle something more than Sun signs. Debbie's book is full of insight and rollicking humor.

Lundsted, Betty. *Transits, the Time of your Life*, Samuel Weiser, York Beach, ME, 1980. An excellent book explaining the process of transits and transiting planets in much greater depth than we were able to do in Chapter Seven.

Pelletier, Robert. *Planets in Aspect*. Para Research, Rockport, MA, 1974. Readable, gives interpretations about each separate aspect (square, trine, etc.) as we were unable to do here.

Sakoian, Frances and Lewis Acker. *The Astrologer's Handbook*, Harper & Row, N.Y., 1973. In this basic reference, you can look up readings on your planets in signs, aspects, and houses, the signs on the cusps of houses, and other information to get more from your chart.